MANTRA FOR CONNECTING
WITH
THE DIVINE WITHIN

|| ॐ ज्योतिरूपाय

परमसखाय परमानंदाय

दादाश्रीजी नमो नमः ||

|| Aum Jyotiroopāya

Paramsakhāya Parmānandāya

Dādāshreeji Namo Namah ||

Meaning:

He Whose form is Light

And Who is Supreme Friend

And His quality is Supreme Bliss

To That Dadashreeji we offer obeisance multiple times.

THE CAUSE OF SUFFERING IS THE LACK OF LOVE

is a compilation of teachings and guidance

MAITREYA DADASHREEJI

A DIVINE FRIEND

First published in 2019 by

Becomeshakespeare.com

Wordit Content Design & Editing Services Pvt Ltd
Unit - 26, Building A -1, Nr Wadala RTO,
Wadala (East), Mumbai 400037, India
T: +91 8080226699

ISBN - 978-93-88930-57-4

This book is dedicated to those

who are yearning for the Divine,

seeking the Truth, and

who want to experience

Divine Love.

Acknowledgements

The MaitriBodh Parivaar expresses its gratitude to all its mitras and maitreyis for their tireless contributions in the mission of establishing Love and Peace in the world. Each one plays a special role in this Golden Era, through his/her prayers, acts of Selfless Service, and humanitarian efforts to uplift the underprivileged, heal the needy with Love, and work ceaselessly to help each one establish the most beautiful bond with the Divine.

We, especially, thank all our mitras and maitreyis who have helped in compiling this Divine book that endeavors to correct the misconceptions about spirituality, bring clarity and guide one and all on the path of Truth and Love.

The spiritual path is about
genuine feelings and pure actions,
and not about high philosophies
or profound complex knowledge.
It has never been about
false ideation or fantasies
that the mind creates.

\- Dadashreeji

Dadashreeji
- The Transforming Presence

Beautiful, deep eyes, looking into which you are transported to the center of the universe; a gentle smile that helps you connect with Him easily; clad in all whites, Divine Friend Dadashreeji appears very simple to the human eyes, yet His greatness and glory can easily be experienced by a pure and awakened soul. Choosing to be born with the illusions of the human realm and growing up in the limiting material world, Dadashreeji has successfully navigated the various challenges of a human life, broken free from the shackles of the mind, and evolved to His Supreme Divine state to set a living example for mankind to attain their true nature of Divinehood.

Born to humble origins, Dadashreeji grew up with a kind heart and a curious mind. A responsible citizen and a social reformer, He opted to become a medical doctor by profession. While treating one of His very young patients, He realized the limitation of man in healing suffering even while offering him the best of medical aid for physical pain. Thus, He began His quest on the Higher path. Various saints, deities, and historical figures began visiting Him astrally. In 2006, Mahavataar Babaji appeared before Him and disclosed:

• • •

"My consciousness is within You to help Our mission of Maitri as The Love Incarnate."

After this mystical encounter, Dadashreeji's internal state started transforming from a human one to that of The Divine. He spent the next few years on the journey within to prepare Himself for guiding mankind. Babaji had told Him that He not only had to lead humanity to the Divine Age but also carve a new path that is best suited for this time – the path of Maitri (Love and friendship with the Divine).

He began to examine the human mind, and He personally experienced all the states of Transformation to realize that He is the Liberated One who has descended to help liberate others. Dadashreeji and Babaji are akin to two sides of the same coin. It is an interplay of the same Divine Consciousness: two forms but one Soul.

Towards the close of 2012, Dadashreeji conducted the first level of His signature **Bodh** retreats. He revealed the Saptaang Marg – the seven limbs of life, through which one can find all the solutions to their daily questions on life. If one understands and follows the seven points of the Saptaang Marg judiciously, one is sure to attain the Highest level of awakening. He also revealed the sutras of hidden Divine wisdom and the Laws of Karma, hitherto unknown to man.

The most crucial part of the Bodh program is the scientifically-proven Divine Energy transfer called *ShaktiPravaah* through which mental, emotional and physical blocks of the individual are removed to give a positive boost to the growth of the soul. Words fall short in expressing gratitude for this most potent boon given by Dadashreeji to humanity, for this era. This process of Divine intervention not only helps uplift one's consciousness but also transforms their minds with improved mental cognitive processing and develops a positive sense of emotional well-being within.

With the vision of establishing "One World, One Community, One Truth", He founded The MaitriBodh Parivaar in 2013 to transform souls, dissolve boundaries, help humanity bond, and unite nations together. He began guiding and directing many youth, atheists, believers of all faiths, and people from all castes and creed to understand the purpose of their lives and work towards it. As a medical doctor, He didn't like to prescribe many medicines for one illness. He would dig deep to understand the root cause of the physical discomfort and suggest appropriate treatment accordingly. Similarly now, as a Spiritual Doctor, when He witnessed the emotional, mental, and spiritual suffering of man, He explored it deeply to understand its source to be able to treat it at its very root. After deep contemplation, Dadashreeji disclosed the most insightful teaching that man has spent lifetimes trying to understand and comprehend. Following the Divine Friend's footsteps of imparting only genuine and pure spirituality, this revelation is the core teaching at The MaitriBodh Parivaar:

"The cause of suffering is the lack of Love."

Being the Love Incarnate Himself, Dadashreeji's presence is enough to make one experience Divine Love. When a candle is lit in a dark room, it instantly dispels darkness. It doesn't make any effort to brighten up the room, but its presence does so on its own. When you add sugar to milk, it naturally becomes sweet. You don't have to do anything additionally. Similarly,

Dadashreeji is a Transforming Presence.

Simply by being in His presence, one experiences Divine Love within them, which initiates inner Transformation to their true nature of being Divine themselves. It is all very subtle, dreamlike, and effortless, the way He works within us. The experience of His Presence is that of Unconditional Love; the mind comes to a standstill, the heart flowers open, expressing itself, connecting us to the Source of creation. One cannot miss the simplicity of His Being and His words. He shares deep wisdom and imparts most profound knowledge with incredible ease and simplicity, guiding us to the ultimate path of Divine Union while enabling us to experience the Truth, transformation and eventually self-realization within.

Once Dadashreeji asked a group of seekers, "What is a soul?" The seekers gave elaborate definitions and descriptions of a soul, each more astounding than the previous, at which He simply smiled. He then asked them, "How many of you have felt, touched, or experienced your soul?" With no hands raised to His simple question, Dadashreeji explained that one's soul, consciousness and the highest of spiritual states are to be experienced and not to be read or imagined about as others have described them to be, because those who have written about them, have never experienced these states themselves and those who have truly experienced them, have never been able to put them into words.

Dadashreeji says, "Before me, many have delivered teachings and techniques for your salvation and liberation. I am not here to repeat them, but to deliver that experience in your heart so that it becomes your own personal Truth."

• • •

He does not teach the seekers in the traditional way with a notebook and pen. He looks at your being and speaks to your very soul. He knows you not only as you are today, or how you were before but also as you have been in the previous life, the ones before that, and as you have existed as a soul since time immemorial. He relates to your Highest Self and guides you from that perspective, knowing fully well what you're experiencing today. However this does not imply that He removes all the problems from your life. Instead, He helps you understand why you are facing what you are, how to grow through it and emerge as a stronger being.

Dadashreeji is a Divine Friend who awakens our Inner Divine and helps us experience the Divine as a friend seated within our own hearts (not the anatomical heart). Dadashreeji loves us unconditionally, without any expectations. If anything, He expects us to grow spiritually and rise to our highest potentials.

On the path of one's transformation, Dadashreeji has laid great impetus on the joy of serving others. In 2013, He formed the **Youth for Global Peace and Transformation (YGPT)** to guide youngsters, help them connect with their Highest Self, and render selfless social and spiritual service to mankind. His family of friends have been spreading awareness on holistic wellbeing, heartful living and organizing various wellness camps to share the experience of blissful love that He has blossomed in their hearts.

He says, "One can know me easily only when one's heart is pure and awakened. For others, ask for the experience to know me. You may forget your questions; I will not forget to answer them," and He lives up to His word to send guidance to each child, but His ways vary. To some, the Divine Friend replies through external signs on the road side or on a wall; to some via messages through a stranger or a loved one; and to some, or in fact many of His devotees now, through their awakened Inner Voice. Redefining the path to the Divine, Dadashreeji is guiding seekers to stop at nothing but the Highest. He is taking seekers straight from ignorance to awakening, self-realization and enlightenment, to transformation, liberation and beyond.

At the same time, Dadashreeji is not limited to the MaitriBodh Parivaar or only to those that pray to Him. Dadashreeji gives complete freedom to each seeker of the Truth to follow any Guide or Master they connect with. He is always listening, guiding, nurturing, protecting, and loving all devotees, any seeker who calls out to Him. He represents Divinity for one and all, beyond all human limitations.

We are extremely blessed and fortunate to be living at a time when Dadashreeji Himself is on Earth. His Presence is uplifting the consciousness of humanity and His Words are dissolving ignorance to direct the mind towards the Truth.

To understand the infinite, the ineffable, the immanent, words can never do any justice. Dadashreeji, the Transforming Presence is an experience of the soul. You may relate to Him as a friend, a brother, a father, a Guide, or whatever comes to you naturally. Simply close your eyes, wherever you are, and call out to Him. Experiment it for yourself. Dadashreeji says, "We have forgotten the Creator Himself and are lost in His creation, searching for peace all over this world, whereas peace lies in the true bonding with the Source of it all."

With a nod of His head and a faint smile, Dadashreeji has removed the sludge of karmas that blocked the growth of numerous individuals. In a bow of the devotee, Dadashreeji has blessed the child with a bounty of Grace to help him travel across this life to the one from where he never has to come back.

Dadashreeji had once shared with the mitras and maitreyis that the most convenient way to reach a distant place in today's world is by taking a flight. It is the fastest medium of travel but not many can afford it. If you travel by train, you will take more time to reach your destination but you will be able to take a few more along. However, if you want to take everyone along with you, you will have to go walking. It will surely take time but the fruit of this patience and dedication will be very sweet. We, mitras and maitreyis of the MaitriBodh Parivaar are here to do just that. Guided by our Divine Friend Dadashreeji, we are walking the path of transformation; transforming ourselves, and gradually, those associated with us. It is a long journey on this path of unconditional love and selfless service, yet we move on, taking everyone along, till we all reach the true abode of our soul.

We welcome you all on this journey back Home!!

Love and Gratitude,
The MaitriBodh Parivaar.

Mahavataar Babaji
A Timeless Incarnation.....

"What's the color of water?" Divine Master once asked. Days passed contemplating on how to define the color of water. The human mind was baffled and lost patience, yet struggled to know the answer. We changed the approach towards the question. Astonishingly, water became red, then green, then blue, and many other shades of color. In all of these, water retained its natural chemistry. The color of water perceived by the human eye is totally different than its natural color, not seen by the human eye. The natural color of water represents Truth, Purity, and Divinity.

The above discussion was one of the interactions that we had during our spiritual interactions with Babaji. The purpose of sharing this example here is to explain to you how difficult it is to define the form of the Divine in the worldly sense. How can one describe the existence of Divine Mahavataar Babaji? Before my encounter with Him, I hardly had any idea about His form. At that time, it truly helped the human mind to accept His existence without resistance. I had no limiting preconceived ideas about Him. It was a smooth transition from the human plane to the Divine. Many stories and mental imaginations complicate things for others to comprehend the simple Truth. So, it is our humble request to drop the perceived false ideas to know Him truly.

• • •

Simplicity is the first lesson that I learnt from Babaji. He prefers to operate without any spiritual titles. Considering it as my duty, I will try to present a very brief and simple description of Babaji. It will ease your spiritual journey effectively, especially if your journey involves Babaji.

Being a medical doctor, should I avoid sharing things that may challenge a rational mindset and go on with limited human possibilities? Will it be appropriate to present things that may only fit well with modern science? After understanding all the spiritual dimensions and the limitless possibilities which exist beyond the human mind, would it be ethical to not to share the Truth with the true seekers? I concluded soon enough and preferred to share the Truth as it is, mainly for those seekers who are seriously and genuinely working on their spiritual growth since long. The spiritual Truth remains unaltered at all times, whereas current logical facts may change in due course of time.

The first cerebral blow that rational thinkers receive is the physical existence of Babaji in a human form. The mundane mind struggles to accept this. Babaji has been here on this planet since the past 5000 years. His physical body looks like that of a young boy of around 25 years. The only cloth that he wears is an orange-coloured dhoti (piece of cloth) wrapped around the waist coming to just above the knees. However, His mystical physical manifestation occurs in various attires not limited to the dhoti. He dwells high up in the Himalayan range away from any human habitat. There are 3-4 disciples with Him who learn and work for a higher cause. He is aware of all the events occurring in the world. The Divine energy has been exuding through each and every pore of His soft Divine body since thousands of years. He has never represented any cult, religion, or specific spiritual technique but only 'The Truth'. He is peacefully resting in the state of dis-identification. He interacts with a few chosen ones to share and teach the higher knowledge at His will.

He has shared many spiritual revelations and incidents of the past. The one that I could not forget was about His spiritual association with His Divine Master Agastya. The major spiritual contribution made towards His unfathomable spiritual state was by His Master Agastya. The Divine Master transformed an aimless young boy into a Divine phenomenon. Master Agastya who received the supreme knowledge directly from Lord Shiv imparted the same to young Babaji. As per the instructions of Lord Shiv, Master Agastya relocated from the Himalaya to the southern region of India. This is where he met this young boy. As a disciple, Babaji surrendered completely at His Master's feet and followed everything that was taught to Him with faith and discipline.

Babaji received the sacred Vedic knowledge, understood the nature of Hiranyagarbh (Womb of the Universe), and expanded into the all-pervading Divine Consciousness. He had the spiritual key to open all the spiritual doors. He thus became 'The Truth'.

With His will, He decided to stay on Earth to guide spiritual seekers and uplift human consciousness to a Higher Divine Consciousness. In fulfilling His role, He appeared physically to many spiritual masters like Lahiri Mahashaya and Sri Yogananda. He initiated saints like Tukaram. He physically guided Saint Dnyaneshwar and Saint Kabir. He taught lessons on Love and meditation to our beloved Jesus Christ. In the15th century, the Sikh Guru, Guru Nanak ji enlightened the world by teaching the importance of a Master in one's life and transforming one's fallen Being into a Divine one. Guru Nanak ji had received guidance physically from Babaji during this period. He taught vedic lessons to Adi Shankaracharya who advocated the vedic knowledge. Divine beings like Sai Baba, Ramana Maharshi, Neem Karoli Baba, and Rabindranath Tagore have all witnessed the same Truth. There are so many such divine encounters that spiritual leaders have had in the past which is out of scope here.

I had my moment of epiphany that occurred unexpectedly in the year 2006. All of a sudden, a Divine form of a young Master appeared levitating in the air. Before I could gather my senses, He performed a ritual, initiating me as His disciple. I had no clue about such rituals, never saw, heard or read them anywhere. The ritual continued for a few minutes and then He whispered a few words as a part of the process. The moment was completely overpowered by the unknown spiritual energies operating beyond the human senses. The mind ceased to respond, frozen in time, the body went numb, and my entire being was infused with Divine enriching energies as if soaked in bliss. The incomplete Being that existed before this moment disappeared, resulting in a complete new Being. The body and the mind took time to comprehend what had happened. I did not share this moment with anyone till 2010. It was a personal experience, not meant for others to know. The then chaotic human mind was transformed into the now peaceful 'Divine Mind'. Later, He revealed the purpose of my coming and guided me to take steps towards fulfilling it. This is probably the first time that I am sharing my first encounter with Babaji. Being with Babaji is 'being in Love'. With His association and guidance, I became what I am. I was That. I am That. I am Love.

Currently, Babaji is working intensively to transform the

human mind into a Divine one. He has directly initiated fifty-four spiritual beings as his disciples and guided them to fulfil their spiritual purpose. This team of fifty-four Masters under His guidance and with His blessing are working for the same spiritual cause. Each had their own unique experience of meeting and receiving guidance from Babaji. Unfortunately, publicly known history has limited Babaji's contribution to a particular form of meditation, i.e., Kriya, and not more than that. It is sometimes disheartening that people didn't get to know Him completely. How can the Knower of everything be confined only to Kriya Yog? But, soon the time will change. Your wait will be over at the right time. Seekers will see and know complete Babaji.

Babaji, being in the Supreme State, condensed all that He knew into one simple teaching.

....

|| प्रेमैव साध्यतां प्रेमैव साध्यताम् ||

Love alone is to be attained, Love alone be attained.

....

Love is the nature of the Divine. Love is the basic element of the universe. It is only through Love that human consciousness can merge with the Supreme Truth and transform into Divine Consciousness. Sometimes for spiritual intellectuals, yogis, and vedic scholars, it is hard to understand the spiritual Truth through Love. Everyone has their own way of discovering the Truth. We can only humbly request you to add the missing ingredient in your spiritual recipe. Hence, add 'Love' as the essential ingredient. You will witness the change immediately.

The one way to add Love in your daily practice is by chanting the mantra of your Divine.

• • •

This is an effective and easy way to connect with the Divine. We are sharing the Babaji mantra with you as given below. One can chant this mantra 108 times daily to be able to receive His grace and guidance for spiritual growth.

···

|| ॐ आदिनाथा विश्वगर्भा

त्रिकाल सर्वलोके स्वामी

जगत्सद्गुरु महावतार बाबाजी सत्यम् त्वम् नमः ||

|| Aum Ādināthā Vishwagarbhā
Trikāla Sarvaloke Swāmi
JagatSadguru Mahāvatāra Bābāji
Satyam Tvam Namah ||

|| I pay obeisance to the first ever Being, womb of the Universe,
Knower of past, present, and future, King of all worlds,
Master of the Universe, Mahavataar Babaji,
You are that Truth. ||

···

Once you practice chanting the above mantra regularly for a few months, you can progress further to chant another yet more powerful mantra that instantly connects you with Babaji. The mantra is also known as a Panchakshara mantra (five-syllable excluding ॐ).

···

|| ॐ अजाय नमः ||

|| Aum Ajāy Namah ||
|| Salutations to The Conquerer of Life and Death ||

···

Regular chanting of this mantra will bring you closer to Babaji. Deep spiritual and mystical changes may happen within, not limited to the meaning given above. Only the Awakened Master can explain to you the hidden meaning of the mantra.

When you receive such a powerful mantra directly from your Master, the effect of chanting increases manifold. In such a case, the mantra is already siddh, i.e., charged and perfected.

Enjoy the Grace at this available spiritual moment! Close your eyes, start chanting the first mantra and receive the guidance and grace! Walk on the path of spirituality that completes you within!

Be like an eagle! The one who can fly high, away from the mediocre and mundane life; the one who has sharper and far-sighted vision; the one who can look directly into the Sun; the one who can protect and Love others under his wings. These are the Divine qualities. Pray to the Divine for these qualities!

Welcome Babaji - The Divine with an open heart and receive the Grace to transform your false identity into that of a true Divine Being.

Babaji Loves you!
Divine Loves you!
Dadashreeji Loves you!

Love and Blessings!
Dadashreeji!

• • •

Prologue

Make me your Friend.
I will walk with you every moment to listen,
guide, and support you.

- Dadashreeji

Message to the World

Dear Friends,

Humanity in the modern age has been focusing on developments in various fields, leading to greater heights and achievements in the material world. The modern age has seen the various ages of reasoning, industrialization, science, technology, electronics, and computers amongst others. But now the time has arrived for the advent of the 'Age of The Divine' – something which we have mentioned to you off and on. The 'Age of The Divine' would continue over the next few thousand years.

The initial time for its establishment on Earth would happen over the next 200 years. This paradigm shift in global consciousness is going to be a phenomenon truly worth witnessing. Many people would realize and identify with this shift in global consciousness in the due course of time.

The next ten years are vital for us, as much depends on the raised consciousness of humanity. The year 2025 is crucial – as it would decide the planet's fate. Following this, the year 2032 would initiate greater changes for the globe and you would witness the phenomenon that all of you have prayed for. Humanity has been given a huge opportunity to 'make it' this last time. No one can dissociate themselves from it.

The current times are filled with challenges, which we as citizens of the country and beings of the planet are going to face. The major shift is still waiting to happen. Our work over the last two years has already started showing good results.

Humanity would be offered opportunities that would help society to grow positively, prosper, and lead to inner Transformation. Denial of these positive opportunities would make one walk towards darkness. You, as devotees, need to understand and realize that your positive and selfless acts would help in stopping the current trend of our society's downfall and instead make it rise to Divinity. Grace will reach your doorstep to help you; but it is upto you to accept or refuse the gift of Grace. The world may or may not notice your contributions. We are not here for the recognition but to continue our acts of selfless contribution, thereby leading to that Transformation.

Our message to the world is :

1. *Get transformed for your betterment, for your inner peace.*

2. *Associate and set a bond with the Divine in any form of your choice.*

3. *Serve selflessly.*

4. *Share goodness with all.*

5. *Radiate Love and Peace in all directions.*

I am here to answer your queries about the saadhana, tapas, and hard work you have done since long to gain the Absolute Truth of Divine existence. It is not a coincidence that we met now – it was predestined. I am *totally confident that each one of you present here, as well as all my devotees living around the world, have the strength to transform others. We will work as ONE to bring about that Transformation.*

Love and Blessings!
Dadashreeji

1ˢᵗ June, 2014 at ShantiKshetra Premgiri Ashram, Karjat

Contents

• • •

Awakening

There exists a silent

unheard voice in all

to discover the Self within.

The one who has experienced this inner calling,

knows Truth exists beyond the obvious reality.

\- Dadashreeji

Start of a Journey

Dear Friends,

My Blessings and Love to all those who share the unconditional Love and Divine bond!

I felt I should emphasize more to enlighten seekers committed on the spiritual path. How do we see the spiritual path? Where do we lack in it? Are we still focused on it? Where do we stand on the spiritual path? Have we strayed from the path? I would try to address these enquiries here each month.

Please be very clear that the spiritual path is about genuine feeling, and pure actions, and not about high philosophies and profound complex knowledge. It has never been about false ideation or fantasies which the mind creates. Many aspirants waste their energies in the imagination of something which doesn't exist, many a time explaining how different they are from the others. When you use your energy in this manner, it will be insufficient when truly needed. This makes you feel tired, and lethargic, and leads to lack of interest in doing anything. You need to save and gather your energies to use them only when and where they are required, and not on things which have little or no purpose in your life.

The confusion of the mind (misguided mind) makes you vulnerable and traps you in the worldly creation. All events that appear now disappear in the very next moment. You extract meanings out of these events, based entirely on your perception of things. You keep playing with this for your entire life, i.e., extracting meaning through worldly events. It is a natural process of human existence. However, the biggest hurdle in the spiritual path is not the 'extraction of the meaning', but believing 'that perception is final'. Please know that there is no final perception.

As a true seeker, one must extract meanings not from the events but from the 'Self' and its existence in the world. You tend to focus more on events occurring externally and very rarely on the internal world.

While walking on the path towards the Divine, one must start being true to oneself. Years of saadhana will be wasted if you are not true to yourself. When you carry false images about yourself and convince your Internal Being that your imagination is real, consider that you have strayed from the path, gone so far astray that it would be difficult for you to come back on the path.

The mind gets easily influenced in the tempting world, which always has something to offer to please you and your senses. You feel so happy and charged enjoying these offers. A seeker or a devotee might get attached to their good deeds, experiences, and knowledge. You start claiming to be a good sevak, good devotee, or a highly spiritual, intellectual scientist.

We start counting what good we have done. We start claiming our good work done for people, for humanity, for the organization. The moment we proclaim our goodness, it reduces 'the goodness' to zero as it no longer remains good. Your claim of goodness that is attached to yourself, your ego, your need for recognition, etc. takes away the sacredness and bhaav of that good deed. The path of Truth or to the Divine is deeply personal and internal. It is exactly the opposite to your claims of ownership or possession of anything in the world.

If you realize this influence on your mind at the beginning itself, you would be free from it in no time. But if you get trapped in it, it may take years for one to come out of these influences, as it becomes a reality for that mind. It would be removed only when the mind is prepared to face the truth.

I would say do not claim to be good or better than others, just be the way you are. In trying to be good, you suffer more. You become the cause for your own suffering. You are all a part of the same Creation – of that one Source. You do not have to do anything additional. If at all you have added any false layers, your only saadhana is to free yourself from those added layers. Here, your dedication, preparedness, and true bond with the Divine would help you.

Allow your inner world of Divinity to grow with every opportunity you get!

Love and Blessings!
Dadashreeji… completely yours…

September, 2014

• • •

The MaitriBodh Parivaar

Dear Friends,

The recent work done by members of our family for the benefit of mankind has truly touched my heart. Through your untiring efforts and selfless contribution towards the higher cause Divinity has been touched to its very core. I thank you individually as well as collectively, all those who worked, those who prayed, those who felt from their hearts for mankind and the mission, those who strengthened the mission, those who participated in the mission's work, those who opposed our work, and to the many who were blessed through its services.

The current changes on the planet are truly worth noticing. Your prayers are compelling me to answer your questions about the coming time for us all. As you would be aware by now, all of us and the Earth are moving towards 'The Divine Age' – free of pain, discord, and dissonance. All that which is happening due to actions taken now, seen or unseen, is leading humanity towards 'The Divine Age'. There is no other choice. What is left is the path to reach it.

To witness 'The Divine Age', mankind would pass through four phases over time to come. The initial phase, namely that of 'Transformation,' has already begun. Many seekers and devotees would receive the message: "change yourself within".

• • •

Humanity's role is simply to invite and embrace the Grace for the transformative change to occur. One need not do much during this period of time. Divine Grace would numb your chattering mind and channel it towards the very purpose of your existence.

Transformation would be followed by 'Dissolution': the process of churning out and dissolving the unwanted. It would happen individually as well as collectively. Those who are well transformed would flow easily towards the next phase in time. I can happily affirm that many members of our family have already been transformed and others are nearing the end of the Transformation process.

The work of the MaitriBodh Parivaar is instilling hope for Mother Earth. Through their daily prayers, selfless and consistent service, the MaitriBodh Parivaar is rapidly forging ahead and growing through its positive actions that would culminate in the long awaited shift and Transformation in the Universal Consciousness.

The MaitriBodh Parivaar has a vision of One World, One Community and One Truth. All are welcome to be a part of this family. Based on current happenings, those who feel or anticipate the same Truth and shift, are invited to become members of this loving family. The bond of Love within the MaitriBodh Parivaar promises the very future we have envisaged. The love of this family cannot be hidden, altered, or limited any longer as it radiates in all directions. I can see a higher purpose of Love we all share.

Love and Blessings!
Dadashreeji

October, 2014

• • •

The Path of Love

Dear Friends,

A new day and a new life!

It has always been like that! What remains the same however is Love. Love – the ever flowing, non–binding, joyful nature of the 'Self'.

The current scenario in the mundane world is that of 'challenges'. It sends off alarms to others due to the worrisome events that are unfolding. Nations are unsure of which direction to take for their growth. The growth and development that humanity has achieved together since the ages past is 'on test'. No amount of discoveries or achievements can provide a safe future for the planet or humanity.

How can humanity grow during this critical time as a single unit? Political boundaries have divided countries, religions have divided people, communities have divided societies, money has replaced values, and families are divided by selfishness. Making it to the finishing line in such a scenario of a broken, fractured, and handicapped state seems, well, nigh impossible. However, with little choice left, one has to prepare and strengthen the Self.

The limited human mind is trying to understand and achieve all that it can. The human mind on its journey has lost its way somewhere; it has dissociated itself from its base. To get back on track and to reconnect, there has to be a way, a path and a new beginning for all.

It is only the Path of Love - Maitri, that can help you and society in forging ahead. The worries and queries of life slough off with the awakening of Love within. All understanding and logic of the judgmental and conditioned mind is silenced when it encounters 'that Truth'. The incessantly chattering mind surrenders itself, reduced to silence, when one witnesses true Love within. As you evolve and grow on your path, you actively affect the world, thus causing a positive shift for planet Earth.

My request to all of you is, care for the planet and work for the planet. Remember, this care is not limited to Mother Nature alone but is also meant for the people around you. Be instrumental in helping society. It becomes your solemn duty to pass Love on to others.

Make the right choices in life!

Love and Blessings!
Dadashreeji

July, 2015

• • •

Selfless Service

Dear Friends,

It has truly been a Divine and blissful year for our Parivaar. Each and every member of our Parivaar has offered their best in delivering the message to the world. Memories of each day, week, and month would always remain with you as learnings, love-filled and cherished memories for a prosperous life ahead. Surprisingly, the year has ended quickly – so engrossed were all of us in seva, that we did not even notice the passing of time. Let this year end on a Divine note. We, as a Parivaar, are committed to assist, guide, and serve humanity.

Let us celebrate this month through an act of service by each one of us. Selfless Service is one of the core values of our Parivaar – something each of us has been following. As you all know, unless you give to society, you cannot receive. The simplest act of service brings profound Transformation in your life. Through seva, not just you, but society itself is transformed. You free yourself from all bindings. Your consciousness is cleansed and purified within. Divine Grace follows and is showered on you abundantly.

It is only through Selfless Service that you become a part of the Divine – there is no other way. You are free to offer anything that you want to the needy. Remember, to serve someone is a feeling within and not just a mechanical act of providing help to the person. If there is no feeling within, do not do it. If you still do it, do not consider it as service.

Know that the service thus rendered for the benefit of others is nothing but your offering of Love at the Lotus Feet of the Divine. Do not consider yourself as a doer of the service rendered. I have seen many people who are recognised as genuine helpers or great servants of society and Divinity. People praise them as large-hearted individuals who help the downtrodden and suppressed people. These 'helpers' forget that their motivation in helping others is nothing but their craving for the recognition they get. It is the people's respect and attention that they look for while doing seva. Many of them remain unaware of this fact, till they go through a critical situation or through Grace in their lives. If personal recognition is the reason for your offering of service, you do not enjoy the result of true seva. Instead one falls into the well of suffering, questioning the Self: what did I receive after helping so many? Know well that true service is a passionate feeling – truly personal and an offering at the Feet of the Divine; do not claim to be the doer. So much so, free yourself even from the resultant benefit that you might receive later.

I request you all to serve someone selflessly – a stranger or a known person. Do not differentiate between people or seva while helping. As the year closes, let each one help at least one individual. End this year with true seva. Keep this seva personal without sharing it with others. Let this seva become a part of your being.

• • •

I bless you all with prosperity, good health, happy relations, and bliss in the coming year. Let there be a showering of Divine gifts in the coming year.

Love and Blessings!
Dadashreeji

December, 2014

• • •

The Divine Age

Dear Friends,

Divine New Year to all of you! A new day, a new light, and a new life! Having passed through 2016 indicates that you have successfully faced the challenging lessons of life and have proved to be eligible for the next phase of time. All those tiny moments of conflict, issues and discord have become insignificant. Critical and sensitive issues, do leave their mark on your subconscious mind as lessons learnt. Remember these lessons but not the issues! Life is a flow, hence flow with it.

This New Year will bring forth prosperous and fulfilling lessons to augment your spiritual growth. Welcome these lessons wholeheartedly and embrace them! These challenging moments are ways and opportunities for your elevation. This year will be one of the most remarkable years to cherish, as it will lay the foundation for the 'Divine Age'. While progressing towards the 'Divine Age', the Earth would unburden itself of all dirt and unwanted pernicious elements. The MaitriBodh Parivaar earnestly urges you to express Love and care for Mother Earth. This year, pledge to serve Mother Earth and free Her of all that is ill and painful.

The last year provided a direction to all. Similarly this

year will help you in taking the decision to move towards the 'Divine Age'. Hence this year, decide on your own for your spiritual fulfillment. The entire mankind is getting prepared for the 'Divine Age'. As we have mentioned time and again, just participate and be a part of this New Era.

The 'Divine Age' is of the Divine, by the Divine, and for the Divine. Being Divine simply means being 'You'. Being Divine does not mean levitating in the air, fortune reading, the mystical, the miraculous, or the supernatural. Instead, being Divine is being natural, discarding your fake identity, and becoming simpler than simple. You are free of restricting judgements, misguiding influences, and illusionary ignorance. As long as you remain in this state, you remain disoriented in life and act in a haphazard manner. It further lowers your state of mind making you vulnerable to suffering. Hence, know that this is the right time for you to be aware of this reality and commence your journey. All of you should focus in unison, on the vision of the 'Divine Age,' and flow towards it passionately.

We share three essential points to remember and practice in this year so that you may face the challenges effectively, flow with life, and succeed in achieving your goals set for this year:

1. ***Learn from past mistakes****: That means never repeat mistakes.*

2. ***Listening****: Listen patiently and attentively.*

3. ***Gratitude****: Express your gratitude wholeheartedly, either internally or externally.*

Keep flowing with the Divine till you are awakened to the reality!

Let there be Love, Guidance, Grace, and Divine (always is) in your life!

Love and Blessings!
Dadashreeji

January, 2017

• • •

Awakening, Self Realisation and Enlightenment

Q-Dadashreeji, what is the difference between awakening, self-realization, and enlightenment? We humbly request you to clear our doubt. Kindly guide us!

Dadashreeji:

Dear Friends!

The ultimate purpose of the spiritual journey is to unite with The Divine - The Source. All beings, knowingly or unknowingly, strive to attain the supreme state of eternal Truth. History has shown us how human beings have been curious since ages and have harmoniously yearned to understand the cause and nature of their existence. The way to know the nature of your being is generally known as the spiritual path. One can opt for any spiritual path. However, experiences arising from its culmination may vary from person to person, as it is always subjective. We advise you to refrain from comparing your spiritual experiences with anyone else's. Liberated souls would always struggle or fail to explain or translate their state into words. Their presence will help you to experience this state and not the words. However, a pandit (scholar) can explain it well but not the experiencer.

Our advice would be not to ponder much on these spiritual terminologies. It will create more confusion than ever, if not understood or explained well. You can address these only when the state appears within naturally as a lesson to be learnt. Your realized Master would guide you further, dissolving your query into a peaceful state. On the spiritual path, your focus should be on the experience rather than an intellectual analysis of the subject. It may give you additional knowledge but not the experience. Now, having explained the nature of your spiritual growth, we shall briefly share the meaning of the spiritual terms you have inquired about.

Awakening means to be awakened to the higher reality. There is always a higher spiritual dimension to be unveiled for your spiritual growth. When you know about that higher spiritual dimension, you are awakened. The purpose of life is disclosed to you. Life becomes more specific. Life is centered around spiritual values of sharing Love and positivity with others.

Self-realization is a continuous process of becoming who you truly are. Energy flows spontaneously and ceaselessly inwards to experience the True Self. The Mind will crave to remain eternally in this higher state of consciousness. If you consider awakening and self-realization together, they happen simultaneously. Self-realization is a step-wise growth, whereas awakening is an individual change. There is a thin line of difference between them. So, one may say awakening and self-realization are the same, yet different. If it is still confusing to you, do not worry, we will simplify it for you.

Now, let us understand what is enlightenment? Spiritual intellectuals have been referring to this term since long as the rare state to attain or to experience. Many have spoken about it, ironically, those who did not experience it. Those who experienced it kept silent, being merged with the deep state of silence. Let us not complicate it, but simply know it well! Enlightenment means 'you become what you are'. Your True Self becomes the dominant force within. The layer of ignorance enveloping your true being is removed. This is a totally passive state, whereas awakening and self-realization may require an active contribution from your side. In the state of enlightenment, you are free from worldly bondage and the mind is tuned with nature. Do not ever assume that you can control your mind and emotions in this state! Your awareness is fixed or centered at the core of your being. You are internally a free being.

Let us try to understand this with an example! If you have visited a movie theatre or an auditorium, you will be able to understand this well. Suppose, you are in a movie theatre, sitting in any random front row. Now, your purpose is to shift back row by row to get a wider view of the theatre. In this scenario, your seat number is the 'state of awakening' where you know and are aware of where you are sitting. The process of shifting backwards row by row is 'self-realization'. With this process, you keep growing spiritually. Now, what is enlightenment here? Is it the last row? No, it is higher than that. Upgrading yourself to the screen projector room is enlightenment. So, the purpose of self-realization is to lead you to the state of enlightenment. The process of self-realization gets dissolved into enlightenment.

Is enlightenment the end of one's spiritual journey? No, but in fact the beginning of a new journey of your existence. We emphasize mainly on this next step of your spiritual journey known as 'Transformation'. The process of transformation is like a circle never ending, and continuous. It is happening right now while you receive this true knowledge (swagyaan). Choose your path and start walking right away!

Know the Truth!
Discover the Truth!
Fly with the Truth!

Love and Blessings!
Dadashreeji

March 2019

• • •

Transformation

A true spiritual Transformation is like the bursting

of a balloon – first a connection happens

between the air inside the balloon

(our little Self)

and the air outside

(the enormity of Divinity),

eventually both merge into one.

Moving On

Dear Friends,

A new time, a new day, and a new year to enlighten your mind through true knowledge and liberation from ignorance. I wish you a very happy and blissful new year! Each moment proffered by the Divine is an opportunity to transform your being into the 'True Self'. As we all move forward, we leave behind painful moments and deep sufferings. Carry ahead only the positive moments, lessons learnt, and loving memories to cherish and share in the future.

Divinity will open the doors of success, prosperity, Truth, knowledge, and Love for you in the coming year. Keep yourself ready to accept and utilize the Grace offered to you. Humanity will continue to go through a positive Transformation creating greater awareness of life and existence.

You, as a member of the MaitriBodh Parivaar, a spiritual seeker, and devotee should keep your mind open to receive the Divine Grace, thus releasing yourself from all binding mental blockages. The coming year will set the direction for the world, defining the steps required to take corrective measures. More importantly, and so as to flow with the subsequent steps towards Transformation, I recommend you to consider and work on the following points.

I envisage that the true Love of life will be rediscovered or reset to elevate one's consciousness. It will happen naturally and cannot be created. This new Love will be internal, Divine, and of a true nature. As we progress towards the age of 'Peace and Love', receive the best during this time offered to you by Divinity.

These changes in life will occur individually and collectively, socially and globally. The changes will be extensive and radical. They may involve a change of location, job, or people related to your life. Flow with this constructive time, accept and embrace the Divine and the positive changes in your life.

The most essential aspect will also be the most helpful tool in these times – that of an 'awakened inner voice'. Connect with it! Pray and express to your form of the Divine whenever and wherever you can, preferably daily. Through all difficult times, never leave this inner connection. Hold on to it tightly and strongly. Guidance will be given to you as an 'inner voice' or 'intuition'. Follow your heart!

With every passing day, week, and month, you shall witness a transformed consciousness, altering the current illusionary perceptions to a higher positive reality.

Remember and know:

1. *embrace a Love of life,*

2. *welcome the new changes,*

3. *follow your intuition,*

The unstoppable and untiring work of the MaitriBodh Parivaar shall continue to grow and deliver 'Truth and Love'.

• • •

Remember, let your heart lead your life – not the foolish limited conditioned mind!

Love and Blessings!
Dadashreeji

January, 2016

• • •

Transformation

Dear Dadashreeji, what is this 'Transformation' that MaitriBodh continuously refers to?

Dear Friends,

Let me help you understand it well!

When you are out walking on the road, what do you see? Your vision is limited to the people walking, narrow lanes, buildings, roads, and Nature all around you. This linear vision narrows your view, restricting you to a specific location. At that moment, you can only describe that place and none other. When you are at a specific location, you act within the confined understanding of that place. Just imagine a bird flying high in the air. As it flies higher and higher from the ground, with every upward movement, its vision widens. The higher the bird goes, the wider the vision becomes.

This entire process of flying upwards with a wider vision is the 'Transformation' we refer to. You can think of an aircraft taking off into the sky. Your view widens gradually. At that height you are not Australian, Japanese, or African, but simply human. Similarly all of you start your journey of life with a limited linear vision towards life, mixed with past ideas and unclear judgments. The world appears real, even though projected through the limited and conditioned perceptions of life, as you have known it.

As you get transformed, you fly higher with a wider vision. Your perceptions towards life become more open, positively refined, rewarding, happy, and all inclusive. The most serious issue of life, all of a sudden, appears baseless and menial. The worrisome mind becomes a happy mind.

Each and every moment of transformation rewards you with excellence and happiness in life. With these moments you develop positivity within, with precise decision making ability, and the resolution of inner conflicts. It strengthens your goals and is conducive to healthy relations. You tend to approach every individual you meet and every situation you face in life holistically.

This process had always been a part of human evolution. A rare few in the past experienced it in totality and hence expressed their true nature. You now label these few as 'Great Soul, Messengers, Saints, Sages, Enlightened, Realised or Liberated Beings'.

Time has been one of the most powerful dimensions influencing human life and its progress. Planetary movements are fixed and follow their path as directed. This unchangeable universal phenomenon leaves no choice for human beings but to harmonise themselves with Nature. The rising and setting of the Sun compels you to plan your daily activities. Consequently you have to plan as per the Sun; and not the Sun for you. You now realise that every evolutionary step in the journey of the universe results in a response by creation. These

• • •

very responses (leading to a change in the nature of creation) we now comprehend as 'transformation'.

Since the evolution of the universe is never-ending, correspondingly, transformation too is endless. Thus 'transformation' is an inseparable quality of 'creation'. Hence with each step in evolution we see Nature responding with earthquakes, floods, droughts, storms, and the like. In a similar manner, the human mind responds with depression, violence, hatred, unhappiness, and such similar reactions.

MaitriBodh feels that with the rapid and major shift occurring in the 'Universal Consciousness', our harmonizing with it requires equal and effective 'transformation'. MaitriBodh talks about this much needed transformation for humanity and urges every being to participate in this effective wave of positive change, no matter where you are and irrespective of your belief systems. Experiencing 'transformation' is similar to being released from mental blocks, traumas, conditionality, and ignorance. You start tasting true happiness, true Love, and true peace within.

Let all taste the 'Truth' of our real nature!

Remember, there is no end to 'Transformation', for it progressively continues forever.

Love and Blessings!
Dadashreeji

October, 2015

The Process
of Transformation

Dear Friends,

I wish each one of you a very happy and blissful new year. The year 2014 has been prosperous and successful, leading to lessons learnt individually and collectively. The coming year 2015 shall usher in a period filled with pleasant surprises and joy.

If you have not yet decided on your path of life – that goal where you wish to direct yourself towards - this is the time for you to make the decision. For many of you, this year would be a life-changing period as the following phase would be extremely productive and supportive of your decisions in life. The more clear and open your mind, the more the help that shall be provided and received. This shall also be a time for the myriad false notions and limitations to loosen their grip on the minds of human beings. You would see people trying to free themselves from all that have been binding them internally. This shall be more of a mental struggle than a physical one.

As the year assesses the preparedness of the human mind for positive change, what should one do to get through it easily? I have mentioned this many a times before. Only you can change yourself by taking the first step. Unless this first step is taken, change is doubtful. You need to be ready within – embracing and saying 'yes' to these changes. These changes are not outside, but within you. Just flow naturally with these changes in your life.

To make this journey more fruitful and blissful, I would recommend you practice the following five points this year.

1. *Receive Positivity and Give Positivity*

2. *Gain True Knowledge*

3. *Earn Goodwill and Blessings*

4. *Saadhana (Practices)*

5. *Service for Mankind*

As time passes, the MaitriBodh Parivaar would continue to deliver its message of Love and Peace to all corners of the world. The Love of the MaitriBodh Parivaar would fill the very air we breathe, transforming humanity and establishing the Truth everywhere.

Love and Blessings!
Babaji and Dadashreeji

January, 2015

Receive Positive and Give Positive

Dear Friends,

One of the most significant expressions of the human mind I have seen in this period of time is that humans criticize, they cry, and they complain. So whatever they express, they receive back as criticism, pain, and guilt. This can never help one grow in life. Instead this acts as a great block. If you are firm and determined to grow in life, it is very important that you be aware of this essential fact needed in this current time.

Receive positive and give positive – the key essential that all need to think about and practice in one's life. By applying this Truth in your life, one can replace pain and suffering with happiness and opportunities. Its practice boosts your growth, strengthening you within. It is simple and easily practiced. It is not limited to spiritual seekers; thus all people can practice and witness the profound change this brings into their lives.

People's minds have been filled with so much negativity that it has trapped them from all sides. One is trapped in the illusionary negative world, reflecting fear, hate, pain, and violence. This negative state of mind forces one to face critical situations, individually or collectively, with almost no avenues left for escape. Until the mind reaches this stage, it doesn't realize the importance of human values. The shift in the current times is slowly creating a demand for every being to practice receiving and giving positivity. This very simple act by individuals will help many be a part of the global transformation.

When you start practicing this, you would start enjoying the bliss which ensues. When you receive positivity, you give positivity which further results in attracting more positivity with a greater positive outcome. You form a chain of positivity around you and your surroundings, thereby rejecting negative thought waves.

Give positivity to all and your surroundings with your knowledge, experience, valuable advice, guidance, skills, creativity, contributions, and much more. Practice it when you feel natural within. Just practice it as a good act and nothing more. It would help in shaping and strengthening your personality.

It has been mentioned in Vedas that the royal swan drinks only milk, separating it from water even when mixed. In a similar manner-one must practice to receive only positivity even though it might be mixed with negativity. That means discard unwanted and non-essential thoughts and thus, receive only the essential positive thoughts.

Suppose you happen to be a part of a discussion where both bad as well as good are shared. It may be a story about someone whom you know little of. What should you do here as a wise person? Gather only the positive content for your growth. There are many such incidents in your life where you could have chosen only positivity, yet you did not! It is not about 'that person' or 'that situation' but about 'you' and what you receive from your surroundings. There might be ills all around, but with wisdom select only the positive. In the end, this would form your character.

Hence, never be a part of either receiving or giving negativity to anyone. Do not complain about wrong happenings in your life. Whatever you are going through is the best that Nature can do for you at this moment in time. If you want better things to happen in your life, select better options in life. That is what I suggest – select positivity. When you start practicing this, you would see a profound change within you. Bees are attracted to nectar and nothing else; similarly you too should see only good and positivity. You will soon notice that as you have now started accepting everything, you will complain less and become calmer, and supportive and find great strength within. I am glad to know that the MaitriBodh Parivaar is walking towards this ideal with great dedication and incessant hard work.

You have complete freedom to select your path of either being positive or negative about everything. Remember all that I have taught, it would be greatly helpful in the coming times. My association with you would guide and support you further, making this a joyful and blissful journey for one and all.

Love and Blessings!
Dadashreeji

April, 2015

• • •

True Knowledge

Dear Friends,

When it comes to sharing good, the mind immediately reaches out to it with no second thoughts. In a similar manner, when it comes to removing the bad or negativity one carries within, there is no hesitation and one immediately lets go without any resistance within. Each one of us is willing to gain something better with more goodness; however, we might not know how to get there. The mind wishes to enjoy the fruits of goodness, the positive and its associated happiness. It wants to avoid the bad, the negative, and the consequent unhappiness. How can one gain only good fruits in life? Is it really possible to experience this in one's life?

Fruits are the final outcome in the growth cycle of a tree. As we all know, merely sowing the right seed does not yield the desired fruits. What is equally important is caring for and nurturing the plant. If one sows the correct seed, but does nothing further to nourish and look after the plant, one should not expect to receive or enjoy the fruit. Similarly, if you are looking for opportunities, positive responses, and happiness in life, you need to take adequate steps to care for and nurture the seed sown within you.

One of the essentials of the 'Self' is 'Knowledge' – 'True Knowledge'. Knowledge here refers not to the knowledge of the world or creation, but about 'You' – the 'Self within'. Hence, true knowledge is 'Knowledge of the Self'. It is that knowledge, which helps one realize their true nature. It is not just information as seen in the current context or understanding of science. Rather it is that knowledge which transforms a being. Mere information confines one within the boundaries of fixed notions and ideas, whereas true knowledge liberates one by transcending oneself beyond notional boundaries. Therefore, I say that real freedom is 'internal' and not 'external'.

There is no criteria or level for individuals to attain, to be able to gain and practice true knowledge. One cannot say that he or she is not worthy or does not qualify to practice it. Such wrong concepts stop one from knowing the 'Truth of Life'. Once, it happened that the son of an outcast mother, Jabala, wanted to attain true knowledge. He couldn't, as neither he nor his mother knew the name of his father or the caste he belonged to. He requested a highly renowned sage of that time to accept him as his disciple. Upon hearing his request, the sage inquired of him about his father and caste. The young boy truthfully told the sage that neither he nor his mother knew the name of his father or his caste. This brought a smile on the sage's face. Without hesitation the sage accepted him as his disciple. He explained that only a true aspirant or seeker can speak this bitter Truth. Hence, do not tie yourself down with a false assumption that the search for true knowledge is only for a few and not meant for you.

I advise you not to run to read the scriptures or spiritual books in order to search for true knowledge. You can practice it in your life. All you need to know is that you are a student in the world. See yourself as a student of life, a passionate and determined student, one who is willing to learn for the growth of his 'being'. Even an atheist can follow this path. Divinity does not differentiate between dis-believers or believers of God. Anyone who is a true student of life will receive this reward. It is that simple!

When the mind is influenced with events or false notions, it tends to deviate from the real nature of the 'Self'. When one moves away from the sun, what one experiences is the opposite of light, viz. darkness. When one starts doubting the 'Self', he/she finds himself/herself in a confused state of mind, not knowing what is right, and might even think that he/she is an orphan in the school of 'Divine Creation'.

The sad part of human life is that it takes years and years to realise this. It is in these moments of difficulty that one starts searching for the path to salvation.

'True Knowledge' focuses your mind on the Source of all Creation – the Self. Anything which moves your mind away from the Source is not true knowledge. The more you walk on the Path of Knowledge, the closer you move towards the Source. With each step, there will be moments of liberation within. These are unique stages of transformation which one goes through, though not necessarily in any sequential manner. You would notice significant changes within, but would not be able to pinpoint them precisely.

Your individual consciousness starts experiencing higher states of consciousness. As you grow in this state under guidance, you would notice the Self expanding further – into the Universal Consciousness. Soon you realize the Truth of your existence and merge into the vast ocean of universal unconditional Love, a Divine union of Truth, Love, and bliss.

So walk on the path towards the 'Source' – with 'True Knowledge'. Be there to receive it!

Love and Blessings!
Dadashreeji

February, 2015

• • •

Earn Goodwill and Blessings

Dear Friends,

The shift in the human mind towards Divinity is making its impact felt at various places all over the world. Questions are being asked by many over the continued existence and wellbeing of human and other life on planet Earth. The universe is changing dynamically and extensively. Signs of imbalance are already occurring within its set system. The Universe doesn't share its plans openly, yet many amongst us have started recognizing the signs of the coming change. You, as human beings have no option but that of flowing with the rhythm of the universe.

Till now, man's sole focus has been on materiality, i.e., material gains, profits, and monetary numbers. Does man think that the accumulation of these material things decides the success or otherwise of individuals? While I do understand the value of fulfilling life's needs as a 'duty', surely the demands of material life should not take one away from the essence of life. The material demands and expectations can never be fulfilled completely and will continue endlessly forever. One can strive for them tirelessly, but surely not at the cost of drowning yourself into the 'well of suffering' and pulling others down too. This state of mind harms you first – and subsequently others. You comprehend it too late – when it has already become 'critical' at the physical or emotional level.

I want you to learn to balance both sides of life, where you are free within; speak compassionately and yet take all actions necessary in achieving your life's dreams. When you decide to achieve something in life, you start working for that specific end. You work hard and take every step required in achieving it. In the same manner, when you decide to be a happy being of future, a blissful, compassionate friend, a helping hand for the needy, or any with such a soul-driven purpose, truly a being of the future, you must get everything ready which would be required to reach that goal. You need to think and act accordingly.

Remember, it is not achieving your material desires that gives you everlasting contentment. Rather it is pursuing the heart's dream and being 'there' that gives everlasting happiness and bliss. This automatically radiates to all those around you, thus transforming them too within – freeing them forever.

I have been guiding you on this path. Hence follow that which is best for you. The changes occurring all around, especially the shift towards the Divine are required and inevitable. Together with the flow of the current time, work diligently on earning goodwill and blessings. This will enrich your growth. It will strengthen you within in difficult times. The human mind would go through many levels of change. Here, earning goodwill and blessings would be of immense help.

You must wish 'the best' for everyone. You can help someone, serve, give or share something that you might have. Remember all that you earn here, is not just for yourself, but *should be shared with everyone associated with you. Hence what you do here is for the benefit of others as well.*

Your prayers work magic in others' lives. Your prayers give them hope to cope with this challenging world. When you pray for others, it brings a smile on the face of the Divine. This is where you earn merit and His blessings without asking for them. These blessings would manifest in your life in myriad ways or forms. You may wish to receive them in a particular way or area of your life, but the blessings might come in a different way based on your true need. You may expect money or a financial breakthrough; however, 'The Divine' knows that which is best for you. You would receive His blessings and Love in such a way that it would 'liberate' you within. Keep your faith in the Divine, your true Friend and Guide residing within you at all times.

With this letter, I would request all of you to pray for all those people affected by the terrible tragedy that our neighbouring country Nepal and parts of northern India have gone through. It has been a sad and shocking event witnessed by the world. Pray with deep compassion and Love for the speedy recovery and betterment of the two nations and their people.*

Know your work and act accordingly!

Love and Blessings!
Dadashreeji

May, 2015

* This was in reference to the April 2015 earthquake in Nepal that killed nearly 9,000 people and injured over 22,000.

Saadhana (Practice)

Dear Friends,

Any individual who begins his spiritual journey, is given 'practices' to start with that are commonly known as saadhanas. Every dedicated saadhak follows his saadhana till he attains his goal. Sooner rather than later, the saadhak starts identifying himself with these saadhanas. This is where you start differentiating your saadhana from others. Hence we see gyanis, yogis, mystics, and such following their own particular saadhanas and practices. Saadhaks might not get the desired results from the practice of their prescribed saadhana initially. What lacks here is the basic understanding and purpose of the saadhana, though there is nothing wrong with the saadhana in itself. Many of you are unclear about the real purpose of such saadhanas which is due to ignorance.

The mind understands, in its limited way, that the purpose of all these practices is to achieve what you want. You assume that when you practice assiduously, you would attain its end. I would like all spiritual seekers to know that your 'goal' is something beyond the human dimension. The mind might not comprehend it completely or clearly. So how would your practice of saadhanas (limited by human thought) guarantee your attaining or experiencing something incorporeal? How would your mind understand unearthly goals while being limited by earthly thoughts? I have seen many of you become 'desperate', rather than 'passionate', in your saadhanas. The reason is that you fail to understand that it is not possible to achieve 'the ends' with mere actions. So how should one walk on the path? If it is not possible to comprehend it, does it mean that you stop walking on the path?

One merely needs guidance in understanding the purpose of the saadhana. Saadhanas are actions that you surrender at the feet of the Divine to convince the higher existence to bestow the 'highest goal' on you. The fruits of such saadhanas are boons offered to you by Masters, Deities, or Gods. It is not your actions that decide the goal, instead it is the Divine will that makes it happen. You see some saadhaks do nothing much, yet they witness an easy transformation on the spiritual path. You focus more on saadhanas, but they focus more on the Giver. The former boosts your ego but the latter humbles you. With this basic understanding, develop passion; do not fall prey to desperation.

You may decide your own path and search for a Guide who can suggest which saadhanas to practice. Your Guide would be the best person to recommend saadhanas for you. 'His' constant guidance would refine your practices and strengthen you within to tread the path with passion. There are no conditions or criteria to fit into, nor are saadhanas restricted to a few. These are open to all. You need to feel natural as you practice the saadhanas. It is only now that you will enjoy your saadhanas. As you progress, current saadhanas would be replaced with new ones. It all depends on how well you work, how passionate you are, and how you connect with your Guide.

• • •

If you want to achieve anything in life, you need to act first. If you possess a material goal, you can achieve it with hard work and dedication. For a businessman working day and night, counting every second to make profits is his saadhana. For an actor, rehearsing dialogues with complete concentration is his saadhana. For a cricketer, playing on the field regularly and with great determination is his saadhana. Similarly when you dedicate yourself to your profession, with passion and dedication, you would see the results.

So, work on your saadhanas with passion and great dedication. Define your purpose, develop your saadhana, and follow it completely till you attain its end. If you are unclear about your saadhanas, ask me within. I will surely give clarification about your saadhana. I would be there at all times, to guide you on this beautiful and joyful path of Love and Maitri.

Love and Blessings!
Dadashreeji

March, 2015

Offer Service

Dear Friends,

This is a wonderful time as I see our message and the Parivaar's Mission reaching many people across the globe. Each and every member of our Parivaar has worked hard from the bottom of their heart and to the best of their inherent abilities in delivering the message to the world. For this I thank each one of you. Divinity has recognized this seva and has blessed you with abundant Grace. Your personal growth on the spiritual path is only through seva. Serving humanity selflessly is a core value of our Parivaar. You grow as you give. The benefit you give others – comes back to you by way of Grace incessantly showering upon you as your consciousness is cleansed and purified. You become a part of the Divine only through Selfless Service, and not through any other way.

On the path of offering seva, I want each one of you to walk with awareness. When you offer seva, it should benefit someone – not for your own ego or sense of recognition. Seva should not be for the purpose of self-gain or to gain others' admiration. Seva should be done because it helps someone. You become a wonderful medium for the service but do not claim doership.

The seva should be offered as Love at the Lotus Feet of the Divine. You are free to offer anything to the needy which you feel you are capable of giving. Do seva without any expectation. Even offer back the reward that Divinity will bestow, thus freeing yourself completely. Your seva will be of the highest order when it is done with great feeling – from the heart. If the feeling is absent, do not do the seva. If you do seva without feeling or as a mechanical act, do not consider it as seva.

Do not judge or differentiate between people or the seva you offer. I request all of you to continuously serve someone, either a stranger or a known person – selflessly. Let each of you help at least one individual. Let this seva become a part of your very being. This will help in your spiritual growth tremendously.

Love and Blessings!
Dadashreeji

June, 2015

• • •

Growing Spiritually

Dear Dadashreeji, does the Divine test us? Is testing a mandatory step to grow further on the spiritual path?

Dear Friends,

Nothing is static in life, instead it is dynamic. It is the nature of life to keep flowing and with this, you keep growing. It is quite obvious that you have to clear your tests to be promoted to the higher grade. Hence, be sure that tests in your life are bound to happen. No matter how evolved you are or how close you are to the Divine, it is inevitable. There is no point in running away from these tests. Your refined and better understanding of these tests will clear doubts and fear in dealing with them. All seekers and enlightened beings have gone through this, and therefore so will you.

Being intangible, spirituality is immensely misunderstood and a confusing subject for many. As a seeker or as a beginner, you encounter many diverse and vivid spiritual experiences through your practices. If you are blessed and fortunate, you may validate your experiences through your Master – a realized One. If this doesn't happen, you start assessing and analyzing your own experiences. Your self-interpretation and conclusions may lead you to further misjudge your state. With this self-analysis, you start boasting about your experiences to others. You claim to be a yogi, a devotee, a sevak, a clairvoyant, a healer, etc. Since, there is no available way for you to ascertain your state, you have to get it tested.

It is like a student claiming to know all the subjects, being well read and well prepared, but fails during the examination and then realizes where he truly stands. If there is no direct source or the Master validating your state, you better appear for tests as have many before you. And 'Yes', the Divine does take tests but they are not for Him to know how worthy you are of His Grace. It is simply for you to know where you truly stand while claiming your spiritual experiences or defining a spiritual state.

You need not worry, as a true state and experience will always smoothly facilitate your journey, helping you to overcome these tests successfully. Your transcended state will lift your level of awareness and enhance your growth further. This upgraded state not only transforms you within, but inspires and guides many seekers to learn and explore their path too. If at all you don't clear your tests, you will have further opportunities to learn and assimilate to enrich your 'Being' within. In all these scenarios, the Divine will be present and will guide you further with His Love and Grace. As long as you are determined and committed to your growth, guidance will never stop. Your relentless efforts and zeal to grow in life will always attract the Divine's attention towards you. With the Divine's compassionate presence, everything will change for you. The Divine doesn't need any proof from you, as He knows all. You need to know about your own True Self; hence the test. Know yourself better!

• • •

If you have faith in your Divine and in His infinite, Unconditional Love for you, you would always pass through these testing critical moments in life fearlessly.

Grow with Love!

Grow with Friendship!

Grow with the Divine!

Love and Blessings!
Dadashreeji

November, 2017

Purification

Dear Dadashreeji, is it essential for every spiritual seeker to undergo the 'purification process' (Chitta-Shuddhi)? May I request you to enlighten us more on the purification process?

Dear Friends,

Basically, the purification process is a systematic, progressive, and effective way to expunge or cleanse unwanted, grievous, detrimental, traumatic, rotten, and other dormant impressions of your subtle body that have blocked your path of growth.

Depending on levels, purification is of three types, i.e., physical, psychological, and lastly, the deep subconscious level. As you move within, from one level to the other, the process becomes slower but more powerful. For the first type, the physical body has its own natural mechanism to wipe away all that is not required. On the psychological front, the mind also has the ability to purify itself from irrelevant and unwelcome accumulated thoughts' energies during sleep. Although one possesses natural processes to cleanse oneself, one is unable to use them to their maximum potential. The reason is that many of you are careless or place little value towards cleansing these vital layers. A proper mindful diet and relaxing deep sleep would provide you with a healthy body and a happy mind. I urge you to include this into your daily practice, thus staying healthy and happy in life.

Deeper than these layers is a deep subconscious plane, called the 'chitta' where all your core values, ingrained impressions, and unique traits are recorded. To understand it simply, this is where you, as a unique character, are defined. This inner plane influences your mind, and further, your body in unison. You are hardly able to access this deep plane in these days of competition and survival in the game of life. One may inherently feel or get connected to this level three-five times in a day. There are no other active processes one can practice on their own to free oneself from past burdens or blockages. Hence, this deep layer remains largely unexplored, unattended, and untreated.

This is exactly where the purification processes help you cleanse and remove the dirt of the past, and thus experience true freedom in life. Processes that are done here are well structured, intense, and are conducted in a way that slowly and steadily release you from these blockages.

'Beej sanskaar' is one of the intense processes that sow the seed of Divine intelligence within you. One starts experiencing a truly worth-noting, value-based, conscience-driven, and inner-voice guided life. You just need to follow the basic preparation as advised by our friends while participating in these processes.

We conduct the purification process specifically for the deep subconscious plane (Chitta) and not for the body or mind directly. However, these integral and endogenous

• • •

transformation processes further spontaneously unfold positive outcomes externally. When you dive deep into your inner world, there is a sudden and huge release of energy. The past latent memories surface up to your awareness. Consequently one may experience transient disturbances in the mind, which subside later into a deep silence. You may feel light within as if something unwanted has been released from within you. There is an upward shift in the energy, strengthening you mentally and emotionally. Notable post this process is that your perception towards similar situations and people changes. You deal with the same unchanged, challenging events but with solutions, zeal, and calmness. These are a few markers that you will witness during the purification process, although not limited to the aforementioned alone.

Remember, the only worthwhile challenge in your life is to change yourself. The rest is baseless and a waste of time.

Love and Blessings!
Dadashreeji

May, 2016

• • •

The Divine

The moment you cross
the dimension of the human field,
what you witness is
Divine Consciousness.
Everything becomes the Divine
for you.

- Dadashreeji

What is the Divine?

Dear Dadashreeji, what is the Divine?

Dear Friends,

The Divine is the source of all creation. It existed before all material manifestation occurred. It is omnipresent and limitless. It is both gross and subtle. However, no words can adequately describe the Divine precisely nor to the point. One can only aspire to comprehend a very basic understanding of the Divine.

The dictionary of the human mind is limited in its ability to describe the infinite Divine despite its plethora of the most profound words. Understand well that the mind originated from the Divine and not vice versa. The Divine existence is not the outcome of the baseless mental exercises that people indulged in. When people try to understand the Divine merely as an idea surfacing from their mental projections, the mind fails to grasp it. It can be labeled as an experiment of the mind and nothing else.

Human history shows that many efforts were made to describe the Divine in their own ways. There were many nomenclatures given to the Divine as were perceived by the seeker. This formed belief systems, communities, and later religions. The human mind is still unable to truly comprehend the Divine. What one gets at the end are various forms and names of the Divine, but not the 'One Divine'.

It is akin to looking at the waxing and waning of the moon. With every passing night, one witnesses the change in the shape of the moon. Do these changes in any way alter the original constitution of the moon? The 'Crescent shaped moon' or a 'No moon' is an observation valid only for the planet Earth, but has no significance whatsoever for the moon itself. It is how one looks at the Divine and defines it. Similarly, the Divine remains independent and complete in itself. Your blame or praise of the Divine does not reduce nor increase it in any aspect whatsoever. The human mind fails in explaining the Divine. So, know that all that exists beyond the human mind is the Divine.

So, does that mean one cannot do anything to know the Divine in one's life? It is possible to know the Divine. What connects you to the Divine instantly and strongly is 'Love'. When you connect through Love, you find the Divine is within you. This is where you don't know the Divine, yet experience it strongly within. The moment you cross the dimension of the human field, what you witness is Divine Consciousness. Everything becomes the Divine for you. Flow with that Divine and nothing else!

Remember, nothing can conquer or possess the Divine; it has been ever free and all-powerful.

Love and Blessings!
Dadashreeji

September, 2015

• • •

Prayer to the Divine

Dear Dadashreeji, what should one pray for and ask as the highest from the Divine?

Dear Friends,

Your prayers and asking emerge out of your current state of mind. The materially influenced mind will ask for wealth, fame, social stability, marriage, job, and so on. On the other hand, the spiritually seeking mind will pray for clarity in life, liberation, inner transformation, eternal peace, and supreme knowledge. Since both prayers are born out of the mind, one cannot distinguish which prayer is superior or inferior to the other. Everyone has a right to pray for anything they desire for at that moment in time.

Let us look at it in another way. There are two kinds of minds that I have seen. One is of a lower grade – selfish and motivated mainly for material possessions. Here, the mind will carry the ego of possessions and will expect respect from others. The lives of these individuals are coalesced out of the identity they form through worldly possessions. Their confined living and closed pattern of thinking block the growth of the mind which leads either in harming others or causing mental depression due to an identity crisis. This type of mind, being limited and directionless, fails to ask from the Divine that which is right for them.

The other mind is of a higher grade, i.e., evolving. This mind is focused and acts to free itself from the false worldly possessions. It strives to search for answers at a higher level, and not in the mundane and mechanical life. They too get confused as to what to ask for merely due to a lack of proper guidance.

Considering the above states, it is very important for you to know how the Divine views this. The Highest form, existence and presence in the universe, is that of the Divine – unseen, yet experienced and felt strongly within, 'That', who has constantly guided, supported, and expressed Love to you, in your most difficult times.

What is it that the Divine wants you to ask or pray for? Is it being wealthy, famous, or a powerful person in the world? As a spiritual aspirant, by now, you know that your true happiness does not lie in the external world, but within you, with your Divine. Being aware of this, why would the Divine want to fulfil your desire? Why should you ask for these mundane things? If the world is the source of pain, attachment, and suffering, why should the Divine grant them?

With the fulfillment of every desire, the sense of owning and possessing is strengthened which in turn tightens the knot of the cycle of birth and death. It makes you more ignorant and materialistic, pushing you deeper into the well of fear, suffering, and ignorance.

Ask for that which is not material, but which will help you to navigate through this complex life!

• • •

Ask for the highest and not tiny things. Do not limit yourself to the small inconsequential things! Ask for the eternal, imperishable, and persistent!

The Highest is the Divine and His Love. It is that 'Unconditional Love' that will nourish your fallen state and complete you from within.

Ask for that 'Giver' Itself! Asking for less than this lowers your state of consciousness. Do not fall down to ask for something that your heart does not resonate with!

Hence remember, ask for the 'Highest Divine Love'. It is the only remedy for all illnesses.

All maitreyis and mitras should evolve further and pray for that 'Unconditional Love and bond within' with their Divine. We, as a Parivaar are here to experience, teach, and spread that Love to all those in need.

Be wise and evolved!

Love and Blessings!
Dadashreeji

February, 2016

• • •

Experiencing Divine Love

Dear Dadashreeji, according to you, what is that one reason stopping me from experiencing true Divine Love?

Dear Friends,

It is your mind which is captivated by the beauty of the well-designed illusionary world which tempts one by offering sensual pleasures. Under the material influence, the mind expresses and acts in every possible way to possess everything that provides pleasure to itself. In the chosen journey of the mind, one eventually finds oneself caught up in the unending chain of worldly pleasures. This trapped mind is what stops you from experiencing true Divine Love. The irony is that you are not even aware of the strong and powerful influence of materialism. You talk about freedom but in reality you are stuck in this mesmerizing world.

Let me help you understand this. What happens to the human mind, most of the times, when you buy a new smart phone from the market? You feel empowered on possessing the most advanced smart phone. You enjoy your freedom to access everything and anything that you wish to possess. With that tiny gadget, you possess the information of the entire known creation. The joy of owning an advanced smart phone provides a sense of achieving something special in one's life. If you reflect minutely, you will notice that you have confined yourself to that metal device. Whatever you received was only the information of the world, making you feel that you belong to this free world. In reality, you have become glued to this dead metal, not realizing that you have been trapped within the self-created virtual world.

You can't experience Truth, and freedom, and understand the real meaning of life just by possessing virtual information about it. You have to live it truly – in the real world. Watching famous cities and locations electronically and visiting those in person are altogether different experiences. Watching sports on a screen is fun but playing it physically is the pure joy. It gives you strength, shapes your character and redefines your individuality with positivity.

Everything around has a purpose of conveying something to you. It is not to bind you forever with that and trap your mind. The trapped mind thinks it is free, but in reality it is trapped within the self-created false world. For that foolish mind, whatever appears and disappears, begins and ends is well within the confines of the world. There is no attempt or even a desire to experience the 'Truth of life'. It is only when you reach a dead end on your path, that you start looking for help, support and solutions.

Be aware of this trapped mind! What you can do here is not only free your mind but also allow it to express and experiment with itself. Treat this mind as a gift of creation, make it your friend, and allow it to be guided by the Divine. The Grace and Love of the Divine will make sure that you experience the Supreme Truth and Divine Love.

Remember, express your Love to your dear and near ones!

Love and Blessings!
Dadashreeji

March, 2016

• • •

Cultivating Divine Love

Dear Dadashreeji, I have realized the importance of Divine Love. As a karma-yogi (one who follows the path of action) engaged in various worldly activities, how do I cultivate Divine Love within?

Dear Friends,

Your true identity is all about Love. It gives purpose to your lifeless existence and meaning to your lamented life. You have moved ahead from realizing the importance of Divine Love to cultivating it. That reflects a seeker's spiritual growth. It is not enough to just know the importance of Divine Love in one's life. One must constantly seek to grow with Love. Many of you stop or somehow slow your growth down by assuring yourself that you have got the best of the spiritual world that may be a meditation technique or a highly evolved Master or a special hidden knowledge. Your scheming mind makes you enjoy this achievement, but inside it silently celebrates its win over how successfully it tricked you. Your distracted attention further debilitates your spiritual growth. You don't even realize it. There is no seeking left to pursue but a struggle to get what you had experienced at the beginning of your journey.

The biggest advantage that you have while walking on the

Path of Love is that you receive constant reminders by your Beloved Friend, mischievously provoking you, saying, "Come and get me!" This privilege is totally missing in all the other paths, especially when there is absolutely no role of Love facilitating your growth. Blessed are those who are able to experience Divine Love within, even if it is for a few seconds!

As a seeker of Truth and Love, you should gather all your energies and intensify your focus on spiritual growth. There are two simple ways, easy ones that can be practised anywhere, anytime and at your comfort to allow Divine Love to arise and expand within your consciousness. One should practice a 'continuous sense of the presence of the Divine' all the time. If you have experienced Love for the Divine even once, have witnessed His Grace, have noticed an unclear, irrational yet evident pull towards the Divine, you are suitable to practice it. Although the Divine is within and around you, you have to constantly remind your mind of this reality. Whatever you do or whenever you interact with anyone, know that your Divine is fully present there. During all good or bad events, your Divine is present. If you are tired of the imperfect wandering mind and want to grow towards the Truth of life, feel the presence of the Divine around or within you. Repeated doses of these reminders will disintegrate your false chattering mind. Your consciousness gradually shifts towards the Divine, liberating you from the false reality of life.

The second easy way is to 'communicate with the Divine' while practicing the path of Love – Maitri. By now many of you must be doing it already. When we say Maitri, without any further explanation and addition, you should undoubtedly know that it is about talking with your Inner Divine Friend.

Again, it is at your comfort. Whenever you feel, you should practice it. If it is naturally happening, it again reflects your growth and bond with the Divine. Effortless communication with the Divine is natural. Your growth will amplify to the maximum where you stop measuring and assessing spiritual growth. You become free, you dance, you sing, you act mad (in worldly sense), and you experience true liberation. Your human consciousness merges into the Divine Consciousness. There is no separate existence but one, only One.

With just these two ways, you can easily attain the highest of all spiritual states. One can still explore more and find out various other ways to grow spiritually. You have the freedom to do so. We advise you to make these two methods a part of your daily life until it becomes effortless. In this momentary life, which is a rare opportunity in itself, not practicing ways to get closer to the Divine, Truth, or Love, even for a moment, would be a big blunder.

Don't allow the Light of Divine Love to diminish!

Let Divine Love through you, shine and glow in all directions!

Know the Truth for yourself!

Love and Blessings!
Dadashreeji

December, 2017

• • •

True Friend

Disciple and the Poisonous River

Dadashreeji:

At Premashram, the Divine Master called His student, Mohan, to assign a task to him. The Master requested Mohan to visit a nearby village, Jyotishpur, and spread the message of Truth and Love. Delighted with this seva, Mohan prostrated at his Master's Feet and sought His blessings. The Master knew that Mohan was frivolous by nature, hence warned him about what to do and what not to. The Master also cautioned Mohan about a mysterious and poisonous Vaitarani river. He instructed Mohan to stay away from it, if he encountered the river on his path. Mohan took it as yet another daily dose of suggestions by his Master and did not take it seriously.

The Divine Master gave some eatables, clothes, and a mat to sleep on, to Mohan along with all that he needed on his journey. Excited, Mohan embarked on his journey to visit the nearby village. He sang bhajans and chanted mantras in the glory of his Master. But somehow, while on his path, he couldn't erase the thought of wanting to know more about the forbidden river. He kept asking himself, "What must be there? What is so secret about it?"

As he made his way through the forest, he saw a young, thin boy of around 14-15 years of age through the bushes. He decided to meet the little boy and take rest as well. As he approached the boy, he saw him diving into the river water from an elevated rock close by. The joy of diving into the river was reflected on the little boy's face. Mohan remembered, "Oh! This is the Vaitarani river that my Master spoke about. But this boy is having so much fun here. My innocent Master must have been fooled by the local villagers."

Consequently, with this frame of mind, he went ahead and met the boy. He introduced himself and inquired about the water. The boy said nothing and instead asked Mohan to join him for a swim. He said, "Why don't you swim with me as well and enjoy the water?" By now, Mohan was convinced that there was nothing wrong with the water. Without a second thought, he too jumped into the water. To his surprise, nothing untoward happened. Instead, he enjoyed swimming in the water as much as the young boy. Internally excited and joyful, Mohan wanted to share this new revelation with his Master and other students. He was proud of himself as he had got the secret out entirely by himself without anyone's help. After spending a few hours in the water, they both came out of the river and sat together for a while. The young boy said, "I have to go back as I can't spend more time here. Someone is waiting for me at home." Mohan also agreed as he too had to continue on his journey before it got dark. The young boy quickly walked ahead and disappeared into the bushes. Mohan was still engrossed in judging and doubting his Master. "How foolish my Master is! I have tasted this water and have swum in it and felt only joy and nothing toxic." As he was ruminating

• • •

over all this, he felt like resting on a nearby rock. He closed his eyes to sleep for sometime.

As he slept, he heard his Master calling him by his name, "Mohan, Mohan my child, wake up, wake up." Someone was patting him, shaking his body, and all of a sudden he vomited and opened his eyes. He was breathless and found himself back in his Premashram. He was astonished to see himself like that. Mohan was unable to comprehend what was happening as he saw all his fellow students surrounded around him with worried faces. In all this only the Master had the answer.

Dumbfounded, Mohan asked his Master, "Master, what has happened to me? I was on my path for Jyotishpur. How did I come here?"

The Divine Master replied patiently, "My child, you did not pay attention to my instructions. I told you the Vaitarani river is mysterious and poisonous. All that has happened to you, was because of that river. You were intoxicated with its water. The moment you were unconsciousness, I felt internally that something wrong has happened to you. With my inner eyes, I saw everything that had occurred and rushed there to save you, otherwise you wouldn't have been able to see us all, as you are doing now."

Mohan was unable to forgive himself for doubting his Master's words. He was ashamed of his act but had one more question. He again humbly asked his Master, "Then, Master tell me, why didn't I feel the negative impact of water at first when I was swimming and tasting that water?" The Master smiled at this query and enlightened Mohan affectionately, "It was Grace. When you left from the ashram, you had a desire to know more and see for yourself the river. Although I had warned you, you still wanted to know more. Knowing that you would experiment with the negative source, God appeared to you as a child. As long as He was there, you did not experience any ill-effect of the water. His disappearance resulted in you becoming unconscious. At the same time, He passed a message to me inside and enabled me to see what all had happened. He allowed you to experiment with your desire and allowed me to give you one more life." Listening to this, Mohan became emotional, thanked God, and learnt the lesson for his entire life to never doubt The Divine and His words. He does everything for you with only one interest, that you keep growing internally.

Dear Friends,

Your Inner Divine is your True Friend.

His association stops you from experiencing the viciousness of the physical world.

Having a bond with your Inner Divine keeps you away from all the negative influences and consequences.

Learn to listen to your Inner Divine and free yourself from all the worries and obstacles!

Love and Blessings!
Dadashreeji

September, 2017

Differentiating the Divine and the mind

Dear Dadashreeji, how does one differentiate between the voice of the mind or the Divine? How do we know that it's the heart and not the mind?

Dear Friends,

Remember, the source of the voice is profound and internal. A strong connection with this inner Source bestows natural and effective guidance. Confusion occurs in the highly active mind. Here, one fails to receive proper guidance, which can help elevate the fallen state.

In many instances, prefixed desired expectations make it difficult for you to receive that guidance smoothly. Your preferences influence your mind to participate in the process of finding answers. One feels helpless mainly during critical situations in life. During such complex situations, the internal struggle intensifies and worsens due to your preferences.

Know that the reasons behind the interplay of the mind resulting in providing altered messages are ignorance, judgments, and self-analysis. These various levels of interpretations corrupt the message of the inception.

• • •

If you have played the game of 'Chinese Whispers', you would understand this well. The message shared at the beginning doesn't remain the same by the end of the game. As a part of the game, all of you laugh at the ultimate outcome of the message. In real life, implementing on the altered message can be anything but good or productive. The altered message would only misguide you to encounter failure and misery in life.

Remember, mainly two things that can help you receive the inner guidance precisely in its true nature are: 'Elevated awareness' and 'Connection with the Divine'. As you progress in your spiritual journey, you would notice growth in these qualities. You would receive direct and non-conflicting guidance.

You can identify this voice well as that of the heart if you sense three factors: authenticity, clarity, and serenity. A very distinct, clear, notable voice releasing silence within is the true inner voice – the voice of your heart. As opposed to it, the voice of the mind is unclear, comes with a second opinion or plan B, keeping you restless and in fear.

Your growth and success lies only with the true inner voice, your heart.

Listen to your heart!

Listen to your Divine!

Love and Blessings!
Dadashreeji

September, 2016

• • •

Offering to the Divine
Best Guru Dakshina for the Divine Master

Dadashreeji:

After completing their years of study in the Gurukul, traditionally, students offer their Gurudakshina (offering to the Guru) as they leave their ashram school with the permission and blessings of their Master. On the day of departure, in the morning, the Divine Master invited all to gather next to His hut. The students got ready and came with their bags packed, but with heavy hearts. It was an emotional moment filled with tears and hugs. The Divine Master blessed each one of them and called each student forward one after the other. His students conveyed their Love and offered their gratitude.

His bright student, Brahmanand, said, "Oh my Supreme Master! You have imparted the highest knowledge of all - Brahma Gyaan to me. Your teachings have truly transformed me into a 'Realized Being'. All through the years here, I have been compiling your teachings and have now woven them into a spiritual book. I offer this spiritual knowledge as a book at your feet. With your blessings, I will take this knowledge to the entire world and help them understand the real meaning of life. You will be known to people through me and my teachings. Please guide me!"

• • •

The Divine Master smiled and called the next student.

Student Kevalanand said, "Oh Kind Master! You have taught me various rare meditation techniques. With your guidance, I am now able to see that the world is inside me. There is no separation - no duality. All are One. Through my hard work and consistent practices, I have achieved that 'Higher state of Consciousness' which is difficult even for devtaas to achieve. After leaving the ashram, I will teach all these secret techniques to people and enable them to experience their true identity. Please allow me!"

The Master looked into his eyes and handed him a broom. He then called the next student.

Student Krishnanand, with folded hands, expressed, "Oh Ever Loving Master! I thought of many things to offer at Your feet like flowers and fruits. But, I realized that the vibrant colours of flowers and the sweetness of fruits exist because of your Grace and Love. How can I offer them to You? Everything becomes lifeless in Your absence and the powerless gets strength in Your presence."

"Oh Divine! I exist because of You. What can I offer? I thought of various worldly things to offer at Your feet. In all those things, I saw You again as their source. I find myself incapable to offer all that to You. My Master! I have miserably failed to offer anything at Your feet as Gurudakshina. There was nothing worth in this world that I could think of offering to You. All were trivial and inconsiderable."

"My Eternal Master! I am only left with this body. I offer this mortal body at your feet. Kindly accept it. Make it useful

• • •

as an instrument. Break it. Bend it and dissolve it. Since the beginning, this body was Yours. How foolish I am that I realised it only now! There is no life without You. Oh Divine Master! Please accept me!"

Listening to this, the Divine Master with tears in His eyes and Love in His heart, hugged His student. The student fell at His Divine's feet and cried profusely to empty his heart and requested again to accept him.

The Divine Master, in His compassionate voice, said, "My dear child, you are you now, a real 'You'. You reflect My Love and Knowledge. You are free now. You can go anywhere as you wish. You will always find Me near you, within you…as you have become Me. Go out and show others the true path of life!"

On the other side, for Brahmanand, Master gave His Padukas and advised him to worship them every day. He instructed Kevalanand to remain in the Ashram and serve the ashramites.

My friends! The Divine doesn't need anything from anyone. Out of Love, you offer what you have or what you can. Remember, the Divine's sole purpose is your spiritual growth and nothing else.

Hence, the best offering to the Divine is your spiritual growth - Grow in Love and with Love.

Remember always –

"I am yours and I am for you."

Love and Blessings!
Dadashreeji

July – August, 2017

• • •

Havans

Dear Dadashreeji, you talk about Love as the Highest, then why does MaitriBodh perform 'havans' (fire ritual) for nine days during this month? Why do you advocate it?

Dear Friends,

I appreciate you for rightly pointing out the message of MaitriBodh, which is Love, and nothing else. Hence, know this for sure that whatever we do, we do it with the sole purpose of connecting you with the Divine. For you, a 'havan' may be an act of an old custom or a ritual, but for MaitriBodh, it is an 'act of Love'. It is the calling of a devotee, a seeker, or a child to its Creator, its 'Source'.

Let me help you understand it better! MaitriBodh, apart from other days of the year, conducts 'havans' (fire ritual) mainly during the nine auspicious days (Navraatri) of this month. We observe that during these days, awakening of Shakti (feminine Power) is at the zenith. It is highly active and is available as Grace for a devotee to connect with.

One of the greatest gifts from the ancient Indian culture is invoking and connecting with the Divine by performing 'havans'. However, one has the freedom to choose any other way to connect with your Divine, as per your convenience, depending on your preference and understanding. MaitriBodh feels that with the help of the Sanskrit language (which is also the language of God) during these havans one can easily experience spiritual elevation.

Just as you witness day-night, various seasons, and time-bound planetary movements resulting in different conditions, you also notice good and auspicious times for one to grow materially and spiritually. These nine days are highly auspicious for devotees, seekers, and spiritual beginners to receive the Grace and Love of the Divine. Since these days express the highest form of the Divine, that is, Shakti (feminine Power), one has to devote oneself and pray to that Shakti.

Many of you observe discipline, dietary regulations, or fasting, austerity, and spiritual practices. It is advised only for the reason to remain focused on your Divine and imbibe the best during this time. Nine days of relentless, committed practices with a prayer to receive Grace of the Divine is celebrated on the tenth day as Dussehra. You celebrate it as winning over evil; all negative and unwanted thoughts of your mind are annihilated by the Grace of the Divine, transforming you into your 'pure Self'.

In short, it reflects your journey of life from unhappiness to bliss and from darkness to Light.

Remember, flow with the Divine Grace to experience true Love and bliss within!

Love and Blessings!
Dadashreeji

October, 2016

• • •

Life's Purpose

Meaning of life cannot be taught or explained;
it can be only experienced through Divine Grace.

\- Dadashreeji

The Cause of Suffering

Dear Friends,

While Dronacharya was teaching the secret and rare knowledge of archery to his students, Shon, Karn's brother spied on them, hiding behind a tree. Amazed by Arjun's perfect hit at the bird's eye, Shon rushed back home to teach the same lesson to his dear brother, Karn. During the night time, he hung a rotating bird for Karn to aim at.

Without mentioning much, he asked Karn whether he could see the bird. Karn replied that he couldn't see anything. Wretched, Shon expected 'an eye' as an answer to his question. He kept repeating the same question, but sadly, received the same reply.

Heartbroken, Shon, in despair, asked Karn to hit the eye of the rotating bird. Karn released two swift arrows in succession.

Shon was stunned to see that his brother had hit both the eyes of the bird in the dark. Shon, emotional and elated, praised his brother for his gifted ability and humbly enquired how he could hit both the eyes.

Karn revealed that with his 'awakened inner eye' he could see and hit both the eyes as Shon didn't specify which one. This story conveys limitations of the material approach and that 'inner awakening' is beyond reproach.

Your inability to find cause for your internal unrest and struggle worsens your suffering. You are able to please your mind momentarily but not consistently. You find restlessness within and out, individually and collectively. Not knowing what is happening and why, you act disorderly, missing the purpose of life.

A confined material view makes you see only one side of reality like Arjun, whereas the evolved comprehensive view of Karn reveals the unseen and uncharted reality.

Here, we humbly share a Divine Truth that "the cause of suffering is the lack of Love". Individual, social, and global unrest is the result of this. The only remedy to heal the individual and the society is to help connect all to the 'internal ocean of eternal Love'. Embrace this Truth and get liberated to experience internal freedom!

The path of MaitriBodh is your personal path to connect to your inner True Self.

You are Love!

Love and Blessings!
Dadashreeji

November, 2016

• • •

The Purpose of Human Life

Dear Dadashreeji, what is the purpose of human life and how does one recognize it?

Dear Friends,

The basic and ultimate purpose of human life is to unite with the highest 'Divine', i.e., the 'Source'. It becomes difficult for the human mind to comprehend what this union means, why one needs to unite, and its purpose. This realization comes to a few, by undergoing various experiences in life, while for some the realisation occurs naturally and effortlessly.

This does not mean that one needs to seek boons or worship the 'Divine' to reach the 'Highest'. One may think meditation, spiritual activities or devotion needs to be pursued all the time, by all people, of the religion they have belief in. However, I would say that this is not so!

You must all be made aware that your birth on this planet itself was caused by 'Divine Will', empowering you to attain the 'Highest' in this very lifetime. You would be provided with the requisite guidance and support to reach 'there'. It is up to you to either accept or reject the guidance offered. Each person on this planet is making their own way to reach the Highest.

Please remember that whatever you are doing is nothing else but your efforts to move towards the 'Highest Truth'. In your efforts, both joy and pain would be experienced. My request to you is not to compare your experiences in life with those of others as they all ultimately lead to the same purpose and end.

When it comes to the specific purpose of life for an individual each seems to be different. For some it may be to meet financial requirements, for some finding healthy relationships, to attain recognition, to serve people, for others to contribute through dissemination of knowledge and so on. You too have your own specific purpose of life, first to realize, and thereafter to accomplish it. Being unaware of the purpose of your life doesn't stop you from accomplishing it. However, it does help to know your purpose of life, as then, you are able to attain it faster.

You would realize the purpose when you connect with 'Divine' within; internal communication with your heart would also help you to realize it. In this, your Master or Guide would help you to realize and hence fulfil it. You may perceive it as a vision, voice, or strong intuition within. Your Master would validate the same even without being asked. Be sure and be aware that all you think and do is moving you towards 'The Divine' even though you might not be aware of it. Hence, whatever you do, do your best, and you move ahead quickly. The will of 'The Divine' would guide you to 'know that Truth'. . . and personally experience it.

Love and Blessings!
Dadashreeji

November, 2014

• • •

Strength of Women

Dear Dadashreeji, today women are struggling at the work place dealing with challenges in a 'man's world'. How should they deal with these challenges? Where should they derive strength from?

Dear Friends,

I am puzzled about how to answer this question, because how can one ask a question about deriving strength when you, the questioner, yourself give strength to all. You are the epitome of strength.

You, a woman, are the very source of creation. It is you, who brought the entire creation into existence. Women themselves are an abundant source of energy. It is the lady of the house who sets the foundation of a family, providing strength to all members of the family. You as a mother, sister, wife, daughter are able to take care of yourselves as well as of the men. This however is not true vice versa.

The happiness of the entire family is rooted in the happiness of the lady of the house. Where women are unhappy, the harmony of the entire family is disturbed. Women have been suppressed and have not been able to express themselves which led to pain. It is important that women express themselves fully.

You are unaware of this Truth perhaps due to your lack of awareness about your potential and strength. Just know the Truth of your existence and you would become free of this ignorance. If you study yourself well considering Science, Philosophy, Psychology, and the Spiritual aspects, you would notice you are far better equipped than the masculine expression of Creation. However, both cannot exist independently as separate energies. The disconnect between these two energies results in instability within.

Please note that it is no more a man's world now. The struggle and challenges are common for both – working in unison is the key to happiness and success.

In the past, women didn't get the platform to express themselves but in today's times, women have the opportunity to express themselves freely and completely. Women are at the forefront today.

An ideal example is the maitreyis (female sevaks) of the MaitriBodh Parivaar who are playing their role right at the forefront.

Make use of the current times for your excellence and growth.

Love and Blessings!
Dadashreeji

August, 2015

• • •

Keeping Away from Negative Influences

Dear Dadashreeji, in this complex world, is it possible to keep oneself away from negative influences? If yes, what is the minimum one can do to reduce the impact of negativity?

Dear Friends,

The human body and mind is continuously under the influence of its surroundings. The identity given to this body cannot survive without the outer influence. It is in the nature of the 'human form' to 'sense' the world around and form its own independent perception of it.

Remember, the famous festival of colors, Holi, where happiness and joy in all the cities and villages is shared by throwing various colors on friends and family? If you go out of the house wearing clean, new, white clothes, imagine what follows thereafter. You do not know which color would be directed at you nor can you guess which friend is carrying which color. Out there in the middle of the road surrounded by your friends, you can't remain the same nor come away clean. Their love and happiness will be amply demonstrated on your besmeared face and your color-stained clothes.

• • •

Hence, it is inevitable that being human and working in the world actively, one is bound to be impacted by one's surroundings. There is no place or situation in life at any given moment in time that does not leave a positive or negative impression on you. So know here, all that surrounds you, influences your world within, thus imprinting an understanding, hence forming a judgment.

Good or bad, positive or negative impressions in your memory, express themselves as happy or sad states of your mind. Here, I want to emphasize that you are always surrounded by all the colors of life – good as well as bad. Both will influence your mind equally and on your 'Being'. It is you who has to make the choices. Please know that you will always find two kinds of friends in your life. One encouraging and guiding you, while the other discouraging and misguiding you.

One wants you to grow, to be true, to be strong, and has the freedom to criticize you alone on your face if required. This will be your true, positive friend! This friend will stand by you in your difficult times with no personal aims or agenda. A true friend will never express his own unhappiness to you by distracting your mind. A true friend is one who is truly connected to you through the heart and will be ever ready to sacrifice for you. A true friend will never look for any appreciation from you, and instead will be there just to guide you with complete transparency within and without.

The other friend is an opportunistic, selfish, and fake friend. This false friend is looking for some rewards through you. This false friend is intolerant to any disrespect shown to him by you. The false friend will appreciate you, hide your weakness from you. He will criticize you amongst others but not on your face. They are associated with you because of your status or aim at winning some favors from you.

Your thought gets influenced negatively, thus harming yourself as well as others. You develop a dislike for the good. You feel yourself slipping away from your internal growth. They keep feeding your mind about someone else's negative aspects; how bad that person is etc., thus mobilizing you to his own side, whereas a true friend provides a true understanding of that person or situation – in the most positive and healthy way – even if it means criticizing his own self.

Your growth and well-being depends much on the people you spend your time with. It is highly essential that you select the right people in your life. A true friend can make and form a great person out of you, whereas a false friend can break and destroy your very being. So, remember, association matters immensely in your growth. Be wise and make your choices. Having no true friend in life is acceptable, but having one false friend can be worrisome indeed.

Follow your heart, speak to your purest 'Divine Friend' within. Guidance will be delivered – above and beyond the positive-negative duality.

Open your arms, welcome, and embrace the Divine!

Love and Blessings!
Dadashreeji

December, 2015

• • •

Facing Critical Situations in Life

Dear Dadashreeji, in this practical world, what can help me to keep going in critical situations?

Dear Friends,

Human life is a choice that you opted for. The only reality that you realize when you look around is that you are a living human being in the world. The breath offered to you by Nature is a blessing to keep you alive. No one can take it away against the will of the Divine. You don't even have to struggle to breathe air from your surroundings. It is naturally nourishing your inner being. So, remember that you are very much wanted by Nature. Every breath that you take is a proof of Divinity wanting you to live in this world. Know this, your being here in the world is the will of the Divine for a good reason. That good reason is for what you took birth, which forms the purpose of your life.

The Divine conveys to you through the breath offered, that you have a purpose to fulfil in this life. The purpose of life is always positive and constructive that progressively evolves into an all-inclusive, higher, and harmonious purpose. The only question is – how well do you participate in the flow of life, happily and healthily? The purpose of life has always been positive. It depends on how you perceive it. I do not see any purpose to be negative as the purpose of Earth's life is for the positive growth of all beings. The awakened and sensitive mind identifies it and uses it for its own positive growth, encouraging others and facilitating their growth. So, your growth defines your perceptions towards your life that you form, whatever it is – right or wrong.

First point I suggest here is to change from your confined, restricted approach towards life to an open one, exclusively directed at your intrinsic growth. This frame of mind will never fail you or cause failure in your life. You grow with it happily, whereby you also help others in your journey of happiness and growth.

This open approach further gives rise to the emergence of the 'Hope' factor. Next point to consider here is the Hope – being an optimist. No matter what situation you go through, Hope is the mobilizing factor for internally handicapped ones. It keeps you driving through the critical path of life. It is Hope that keeps you alive. No hope is no life. Hope gives you a direction, a reason to live, a foundation to build, fuel for success, and a purpose to fulfil.

Hope is like a first ray of the day, gradually transforming into the sunny day – the day of all possibilities, prosperity, and success. Keep the doors of your mind open and allow that first ray of light to enter within you, creating a space for that last left Hope! As you grow, this hope will expand into the brightness of joy and Love. Soon, you witness a life that you had dreamt of or conceived before. Hence, I say, be ready to walk through the path of life with Hope and a firmly well-directed mind. Love and success become your friends.

Remember, you grow in life as you flow easily with the Divine!

Love and Blessings!
Dadashreeji

April, 2016

• • •

Challenging Destiny

Dear Friends,

The human mind generally tends to anticipate and accommodate itself with destined forthcoming outcomes. In fact, it focuses more on destiny than what's happening now. With this one word 'destiny' you, in a way, try to define and limit your life. Your mind tries its best to know what will happen in the future. This tiring and distressing mental struggle is further exacerbated by others around you. Parents, friends, and professionals jump into it. Fortune tellers and chart readers systematically, and sometimes accurately, predict a few events of your life. The perplexed and lost mind starts re-adjusting with what is foretold.

Many start visiting spiritual masters or realized beings to know more about their life. Unfortunately, many believers are misguided or disappointed. Somehow, true Knowledge is missing for people to access and absorb solutions for their worries. It happens when spiritual knowledge is delivered as a product of the company. Discrimination between the real and unreal is compromised, causing more confusion and complications for seekers and beginners. The most confused lesson of life is about karma and the associated destiny factor. Hence, let us simplify and understand this concept well.

Consider a petrol station as your total karma and the petrol filled in your car as your destiny. With a full petrol tank, you can travel to your desired location. Your mind, as a driver, will know the destination and will help you reach there. Hence, in simple terms, destiny is the result of the past. Karma are the recorded and ongoing actions of one's journey, and in the time dimension, they flow from the past to the future.

In the name of destiny, the ignorant mind may limit itself, blaming the self or others. It misses the opportunity of using free will to explore and enjoy the journey. Out of fear of losing the focus of the destination, one may not exercise the power of free will. The ignorant mind may restrain itself from evolving on this beautiful and spiritually rewarding planet. However, it is always the individual's choice to practice what they feel is right.

We do not believe in life which is innately confined and further strangulated by the predicted and pre-fixed events of life. Friends, life has much more to offer than what your mind can ever imagine. Your birth here on this planet is not to travel or drug yourself from birth to death. It is about the quality of life you enjoy throughout your journey. It is about Love, bonding, joy, friendship, togetherness, and many happy things in your life. Life is not about moving from point A to point B; instead it is about Love and freedom. It is not about how much you achieve in life, but about Love and freedom you experience within. Do you? We mean now.

Life does carry something from the past, which are only a few karmic points. To scale it for your understanding, it is only 20% of your entire life. Somehow, you design your life only *around this figure and forget that you have a further 70% to enjoy under the privilege of free will. You could have done or can productively do better in life with this knowledge. Erase your past that is lingering in the mind, look at what you have at the present time and work with it. Don't worry about the destiny factor; those who predict, can only do so upto 20%*. With your dedication and relentless efforts, pre-fixed events can also be changed if you really need to. Hence, destined events are also changeable. Hereon, do not blame your destiny, If you want to, then blame your efforts. Today is the day which gives you immense opportunity to change your life, and there is absolutely nothing which can stop you from doing so, not even your destiny.*

Explore and enjoy your life!

Love and Blessings!
Dadashreeji

* To know about the remaining 10% of balance points, please write to us: **info@maitribodh.org**

Life Positive Magazine, October 2018

Using Right Words

Dear Friends,

Love!

My message for the current times and moving forward for all devotees is to work mindfully on the language you use while reaching out to others. However, having said this, the mind is skeptical in understanding the importance of this message and language in today's time. It doesn't understand until it experiences some lessons in life. I feel it is one of the most necessary corrections that human beings should practice urgently at this moment in time. This is an eminently effective, doable, and practical tool to heal oneself and one's relationships.

All that humans have in their hands to modify any bad situation into good, is through language. Here, language doesn't refer to any national or regional dialects. It is all about how you approach people in the best, effective, healthy, and positive manner using the right words.

Understanding any situation that occurs in your life depends on the language used. Hence, the good and bad experiences of such situations are derived from the interactions you have with people. We always point fingers towards others, claiming that they are entirely responsible for the bitter experience derived from any conversation.

As a true seeker of spiritual growth in your life, correct your own Self first. Thus, bring about the best in any given situation; otherwise it will lead to struggle, pain, and suffering.

Most of the problems of life will be resolved by just correcting one's approach and using the right words. Words should reflect kindness, Love, care, peace, and friendship. One should avoid any disrespectful, harmful, or disturbing words towards others and the Self.

My only request to you is to continuously keep refining your words till they become Love and Divine. With this simple act of changing your approach with the help of right words and language, you can transform your life externally as well as internally. This is directly under your own control; think seriously of this change.

Start this change with yourself first, and thereafter, teach others to experience this transformation in the lives of many. All members of the MaitriBodh Parivaar should practice mindful speaking as a matter of priority, thus taking a step forward towards establishing the Divine in everyone's heart.

Love and Blessings!
Dadashreeji

November, 2015

• • •

Dream Small and Receive Abundant Power

Dear Friends,

So, what's the current trend? Is it earning money or buying a new house or a car? All over the world, a common phenomenon that is widely observed, in majority of the population, is 'More and Big'. People have outdone themselves in setting goals for their lives. There is no more a race to earn money or buy a property but to go big and achieve more. The question is "How will I make a long lasting impact at a larger scale?" Today's man is set to win the entire world. Will he?

Human mind that is driving the whole world has got big dreams. Dreams to achieve more and more, with reasons unknown. Stretching yourself end-to-end to get everything from this world will never give you true happiness and peace within. It has never happened in the past and will never happen in the future. This competition of achieving big dreams is killing the innocent, Divine child residing in your heart. Man is losing the meaningful purpose of life. You get disconnected from pure human emotions that are the foundation of human life. Man is ready to harm others, mainly their potential competitors, to prove their high standing in the society.

Many big dreamers aggrandize to prove their supremacy of opinions and beliefs. At the end, life becomes more mechanical than natural with no emotions or true connections. In an effort to achieve big dreams, you miss experiencing the true essence of life. You remain devoid of experiencing Love, bond and real fun in life. There may or may not be a big impact in the world by you, but surely because of constant worry, there would be a detrimental impact on your mental and physical health. If you are experiencing any of these, that's an alarm to change yourself.

All your high and big dreams somehow appear unrealistic, whereas small dreams are always realistic and achievable. Dreaming small doesn't mean to curb your growth or compromising with your potencies. Small dreams don't make you small in the world. Your purpose of life will never fade away. By standing in Mumbai city, it is impossible to view the peak of the Eiffel Tower of Paris. You have to keep moving ahead city-by-city, country-by-country to reach there. And that sounds realistic and achievable.

When you travel by airplane, what do you do? Do you exchange seats with the captain of the plane and ask him, "I have bought the ticket and I know where to go, so let me operate?" Does that happen? Your job is to sit in the flight and follow instructions as suggested. Destination of the flight is set. Even if you sleep, you will reach there. Have faith in the pilot! You can't do anything during turbulence but the pilot can. If you are adventurous to display your smartness during turbulence, you will harm yourself first. Instead, you should make new friends, share your experiences, and help each other. So, my friends, your big dream of life

• • •

will be achieved automatically, you just have to follow the instructions imprinted in your heart.

What you see closest is the small dream of your life to work towards. Please check your dream! It should not arise out of competition but should be your own, from the heart. With your qualities, good team, and powerful energies, you can achieve it. With small dreams, you are at ease with yourself, which further uninhibitedly enables oozing of innate talents. You become natural with reinforced positive energies. The most precious reward that you receive by achieving small dreams is an opportunity to experience Love and true happiness with your dear ones.

Hence, relax your mind! Achieve the closest dreams and share happiness with others! In return, you will receive abundant power and Love, fulfilling your heart and enriching you for further growth in life.

Love and Blessings!
Dadashreeji

Life Positive Magazine, March 2018

• • •

Fulfilling Dreams

Dear Dadashreeji, how do we fulfil our dreams even as we work in our daily practical life?

Dear Friends,

All that you desire or dream of is within the realms of the physical world. There is nothing that one may wish for, which is beyond this world. All that which is experiential and achievable will be of this life and this world itself, even though one may feel or encounter conflicting paths as 'dreams vs. practical day-to-day life'.

No matter which dreams you wish to fulfil, and irrespective of their conflicts with mainstream life, you have to prepare yourself completely, both internally as well as externally to be able to experience this in reality. How can you practice this?

By possessing five essential qualities within that will allow you to live your dream in this life itself.

1. *Passion*

Passion is your natural state. Your thoughts, energies, and actions get automatically focused and pointed towards that which is your passion. You do not have to force yourself to be passionate about something. Passion is ingrained in you.

Your dreams are the passion-driven purpose of your life. The very nature of passion is always positive and harmonious. A passionate heart will never compromise with aberrant, unproductive, or materialistic attractions.

It offers you an attitude of continuously moving forward and never stopping in life.

2. **Devotion**

After having identified your passion, the most essential quality required is that of devotion towards accomplishing your dream. Your dream remains as an imagination unless you wake up and experience it as reality. That is what devotion does to you. It wakes you up to turn your dreams into reality. To put it simply, devotion is an unflinching commitment towards your dream. You gain a single–pointed focus to walk on this challenging yet fulfilling path.

Allow yourself to flow smoothly with devotion! A boon will be bestowed upon you.

3. **Seek Guidance**

When one firmly decides their path to pursue their dreams, it is only proper guidance that enables him/her to accomplish those.

Although you are aware of your passion, without right guidance, it is difficult, or rather impossible, to step further. Not knowing what to do in life or knowing what to do in life but without proper guidance, are both equally ineffective and unproductive states of the mind.

The lack of proper guidance disorients the mind, making

you incapable of achieving your vision of life. It paralyzes the mind in its decision-making ability, especially during critical and difficult situations. You may be well aware of this dilemma when you enter a shop to buy clothes. You know what happens to your mind. Various options are offered to tempt you. Not knowing what to buy causes struggle and confusion. Unclear desires and a restless mind may lead to wrong choices and wrong decisions. This confusion is not only limited to purchasing new things but also to important decisions of your life. Being exposed to the competitive and challenging nature of the material world, your mind starts wandering, thereby succumbing to the pressure. This is where a confined and stuck mind needs genuine nurturing and guidance.

You are just required to convey your need out there to the universe loud and clear! Let your expressions compel the Divine or the Creator to provide guidance in any manner required to elevate you. When you identify the guidance thus offered, be ready to receive it. You must possess an open mind, and nothing else, to receive that Divine Guidance. Freely embrace that path defining guidance. You must discard all acquired layers of the false identity to liberate your potent and powerful energies.

Guidance is the force that paves the way towards your goal; it bridges the gap between you and your vision of life.

Hence, seek that guidance to restore your true connection with your inner Higher Self! There cannot be a better day than Guru Purnima for this purpose. Coincidentally, this month's day of the Full Moon is blessed with the occasion of Guru Purnima. You can derive guidance, growth, and fulfillment on this auspicious day. It is the day to express your gratitude to all those who guided you or blessed you to attain growth and happiness. Gratitude towards your teachers and your Guide will further extract blessings in your life. You can smile and shed tears of joy and happiness in connecting with your own Higher Divine. This day is yours and this day is of your Guide.

Experience this blissful Divine connection!

4. *Rewarding Patience*

Patience is not about slowing your pace of work or diluting your passion towards work, but in fact, it is about providing a well–controlled and focused approach to accomplish your dream.

Patience is one of the qualities of your heart.

One of the most beneficial and essential gifts that patience offers you is enabling you to exchange unwanted and unproductive thought forms with success and happiness. In this way, patience teaches you to shed off the past associated memories and attachment blocking the path of your vision. Hence, remember this, success and growth do not come unless you give up your past to embrace the enriching vision of this one life that you have.

Patience, being one of the vital qualities of the core being, provides unshakable and stable roots extensively gravitating towards the vast ocean of enormous power.

Therefore, we urge you to practice patience and receive growth.

5. *'The Flowering Awareness'*

Awareness is akin to discernibly observing all around in a well-lit room with open eyes. One may blame the situation or fate if one finds oneself in a closed dark room. Here, desperately looking all over with open eyes in darkness becomes a misery. However, keeping your eyes shut in an open, bright, light field will be insanity. Nothing much can be done for the insane state except imparting friendly requests and wise guidance. However, there is a possibility of curing one's 'miserable state'. One can mould this fallen state into a liberating and joyous state. One can experience this by facilitating evolution of one's awareness.

The flowering of awareness is widening the boundaries of one's field of cognizance. It is an ongoing process of expansion of one's consciousness. This flowering heads to abundance and absolute fullness.

Awareness is 'being consciously present' or 'witnessing that to be perceived'. As awareness expands and deepens, you are empowered with greater wisdom, inner guidance, and Divine intellect.

Remember, all your actions and reactions are directly influenced by and related to your state of awareness. The lower the state, the more futile the action. The higher the awareness, the more fertile the action. Hence, help yourself to elevate the state of your awareness to blend into the all-powerful and all-loving consciousness.

Offer your prayers to accomplish the vision of your life with devotion!

• • •

The Divine shall eagerly respond, instilling Love in your heart and a smile on your face.

Love and Blessings!
Dadashreeji

June – August, 2016

• • •

Challenges in Life

Dear Dadashreeji, why is it so difficult to get what you want in life or to do what you Love the most in life? Why are there obstacles blocking my happiness and Love of life?

Dear Friends,

There is nothing in this world that is difficult as you have inferred. Situations sometimes become more complicated than expected. You are unable to keep pace with the sudden changes as you lack a proper or complete understanding of the situation. These adverse situations impact and challenge your wisdom and ability. Somehow, you fail to comprehend the right message during these difficult situations. Due to fear, you confine your growth and withdraw from everything. Before falling into such a low state and getting trapped in it, you need to wake up to reality and rise above such difficulties. Once you are aware of your downfall, you will find ways to come out of this limiting state.

When you are absolutely clear and sure of your passion, the purpose or Love of life, nothing will stop you from attaining it or deflect you from your path by even an inch. Look at the bees! They fly and gather the sweet nectar available in flowers. Nectar is their life, the Love and purpose of their existence.

They drink and store it. They are never in doubt about their need but are focused in fulfilling their purpose of life. For the bees, there are no adverse seasons, no strong winds stopping them nor flowers resisting from letting go of their sweet nectar. Keep your faith! Your Love will help you to find the way.

When you face difficult and challenging moments in life, your fears and weaknesses are brought to your awareness. You probably did not notice their existence within you all these years. These situations give you the opportunity of becoming aware of your imperfections within. Take this opportunity as a boon or a Divine gift! Unnoticed fears and weaknesses are like an undetected cancer, which once active, will damage positivity and end everything. Hence, welcome these challenging situations in life and face them with your strengths and qualities.

Your Divine makes you face these difficult situations so that you learn and grow as a 'being' to fulfil your purpose of life. That means you will be tested as per your passion or purpose of life. Considering an example of a car, a train, and an aeroplane, you can immediately understand that the power required to run each of their engines is higher respectively. The higher the mode of transport, the higher the power required. So, understand here that the intensity of the situation or map of life is designed based on the purpose of your life.

Having said this, you should also know that everyone's path is unique. One doesn't mandatorily need to go through hardship. Similarly, you do not have to manufacture difficulties in life and claim how high the purpose of your life is! Sometimes, people fake and declare to be a victim. This fake mask will never help you to grow truly in life. Along with it, you also remain devoid of Divine Grace and guidance. Hence, we constantly request you - be natural! Be what you are!

"Higher goals in life don't get achieved easily!"

"Remember, difficulties in life demand better and higher of you."

Love and Blessings!
Dadashreeji

February, 2017

• • •

Path of Life
Get Up and Keep Walking!

Dadashreeji:

Everyone at the ashram was busy in the preparation for the twelve yearly Shiv Puja. Merely attending this spiritual festival was a sign of good fate and victory for kings. Many sanyaasis hadn't slept well for days. Weary but still energetic, sanyaasis were following their Master's instructions. Some of them joined work in the kitchen, some invited guests, some cleaned the ashram, and some were absorbed in other rituals. Brahmanand was taking care of the rituals. Being knowledgeable about the work, he could guide many.

Just four days before the Puja, The Divine Master was explaining about the importance of the Puja as many were new in the ashram. Everyone was glued to His sweet voice. He mentioned the mystical flowers available in the nearby forest, Dharmaranya. With increasing curiosity, all present were excited. But the real challenging work was yet to come. He further added that Dharmaranya was one of the most difficult forests that one could hope to pass through successfully. "This forest has many deceptive paths where one can easily go astray. One can still succeed in getting the flowers by being focused and determined throughout the journey." The Master appointed Brahmanand to lead and guide a team of six students. Brahmanand happily accepted the task as he knew these flowers were essential ingredients for this auspicious Puja.

He reiterated his Master's instructions to the fellow students. Taking their Master's blessings, they embarked upon their journey to Dharmaranya under Brahmanand's guidance. The other students were excited and were talking about the various spiritual topics taught in the recent classes at the ashram. Reticent Brahmanand did not pay heed to the discussion initially, and asked everyone to make a queue and remain in the group. The shady and dark forest had complicated their work as they were not able to see the path clearly. The short, curving, and narrow dense paths confused them all. Brahmanand was quick and walked fast through the forest with little interaction with the others. His friends sensed Brahmanand's arrogance and decided to walk at their ease. Brahmanand was aware of completing this task early as he had to be back in the ashram within two days. If he had walked with them, it would have taken at least five days to come back to the ashram. He had something else on his mind. As the students marched, they suddenly realized that their guide friend was missing. They looked everywhere to find Brahmanand but in vain. All were bewildered and disoriented, not knowing their whereabouts nor where to go.

After two days of their journey, on the third morning, all students along with Brahmanand returned to the ashram. The Master was glad to see them all together and enquired about their health and directed them to store all the mystical

• • •

flowers in a vessel filled with water specially prepared for the flowers. The Master noticed a discreet silence amongst His students.

The same day, The Master during the evening satsang (a spiritual gathering), asked them to share their experiences of the journey. Brahmanand broke his silence and informed everything that had happened during their journey. Due to the non-seriousness of his fellow students, he had decided to go ahead alone and collect the divine flowers.

Master asked Brahmanand, "Why did you consider them non-serious for the task assigned?"

Brahmanand replied, "Dear Master! I noticed them spending extra time at their liberty on three things. That convinced me about the fact that they were not serious for the divine task. Having prolonged meals, resting, and talking about various spiritual topics were the three things. They spent more time on these than required. None of them were focused on their duties at that moment. I instructed them repeatedly in detail but nothing seemed to help. I had no choice but to follow the words of The Divine."

That profound observation of Brahmanand impressed many students. Everyone felt the importance of time and commitment towards their duties. The Master turned towards the accompanying students, and asked them with affection, "Then, how did you all come together with Brahmanand?"

One of the students, Mohan, narrated the event. "Dear Master! We noticed arrogance in Brahmanand, hence we continued the journey at our comfort. But when we realized that we had lost him and had no way to go anywhere, we were in despair at our foolishness. We spent a night without any idea where to go further. The next day we still continued on our path without any definite direction. All of us were looking for Brahmanand with a hope that we may see him with Your Grace. At that moment we saw him walking deep in the forest, a few kilometers away from us. He had collected the mystical blue lotus flowers with shining petals for the puja. He was very far from us but somehow we could see him through the bushes. Seeing his physical body, seen from afar, helped us take the path in the right direction. Although we were unable to communicate, we still made our way till we met him. Just by following him, we came out of that miserable situation. We did not inform you of all this as we were ashamed of ourselves."

The Divine Master, out of the treasure of infinite knowledge that he had, had shared one more lesson to be learnt by all the students. He praised Brahmanand and said, "Students, this example helps us understand the importance of walking on your path of life. People may criticize you, blame you, or condemn your actions but you should never stop walking ahead in your life. If you look at it from the point of view of those students who lost the path, it was very crucial for them to see someone guiding them. No matter what happens in your life, keep walking ahead. You may guide hundreds, thousands, or many more than that who have lost their path. Be the light for many! This will happen only when you don't stop in life but keep walking, keep walking and walking!"

The lesson filled today's gathering with deep, unending

silence within and without the ashram. All were speechless and merged entirely in the Love for their Divine Master.

Share and send Love to all our friends!

Love and Blessings!
Dadashreeji

October, 2017

Help Yourself and Others

Dear Friends,

Everyone is so busy in today's world in achieving their dreams and running their family that they get locked into a never-ending competition, extracting all that is positive and Divine within. Eventually, depleted of positive energy, the human mind experiences confusion, depression, and pessimism. This, in turn, creates an unhealthy and inharmonious society. Not only does it hamper the positive growth of society but it also endangers the very existence of community and all manner of species.

The situation is so bleak that there are times when no help seems forthcoming from any direction; you cannot discern a single ray of hope that would give you the opportunity to transform your life. It is like being thirsty for days and months without finding a single drop of water, let alone drinking it. What can one do in such a fallen state of mind? How can you help someone if you yourself are devoid of help?

What are those ideal actions one must take here?

– Spread and share positivity.

– Encourage goodness in society.

– Guide others towards the Highest Truth of life.

• • •

This is the minimum you can do to help yourself and others as well. It is the best remedy to heal the vitiated mind. By showing hope you provide an opportunity for others towards positivity in life. With these actions of yours, the all-pervasive transformation will work on you as well. What is most important is to take initiative towards it!

My Love, Blessings, and all-time support!
Dadashreeji

Life Positive Magazine, May 2016

• • •

Our True Nature

Dear Dadashreeji, am I, as an individual, complete in myself, or do I need someone or something else to complete me?

Dear Friends,

Yes, you were and you are complete as a being. There is absolutely no doubt about it. It is like an outer hard shell of a coconut asking another nearby coconut, "How could you have nourishing Divine water within you and I don't?" It replies, "You and I are one; both carry the Divine water." This is what exactly reflects in your spiritual journey. Hard outer shell of the coconut signifies your conditioned, misguided, and restless mind.

Even if you happen to know or hear or read that you are that pure consciousness, you fail to experience it by your own efforts. Having the Divine within yet being unaware, you look for it outside in the world and strive to possess it. You forget to realize that someone and something is within you.

Now, the next query is, how to experience it or feel complete within? Your ignorant Self or false 'I' doesn't allow you to connect to the inner pure Divine consciousness. In one way, it builds a huge and firm wall between your mind and the Divine. To be precise, your conditioned mind, ego, and attachment block your path to experience your true nature. The most difficult and hard part is the spiritual ego. The more you try to deal with it, the stronger it becomes. Hence, considering your inability to experience your 'Inner Divine' due to your mind's play, you have to think of another way to be there.

However, it is still possible to experience that pure Divine within. It happens very rarely once in an age or in thousands of years. And, then you categorize them as 'special beings', i.e., 'Incarnated ones'. Don't get into it to know why as this will be your next query, helpless that you are by the nature of your mind. Nevertheless, know this as a Divine play! If you experience that Truth effortlessly within, knowing that you are Divine, you will be considered as an 'incarnated being'.

If not so, the only way is to find that Divine outside. This is why many of you look for that Divine in statues and forms that is absolutely fine and natural to begin your journey with. Only someone who is experiencing that Divine within, or is in that higher realized state, can guide you. His presence, Grace, and guidance will help you to connect to your inner Divine. Annihilating false conditions, ego, and attachment, He liberates you to experience Divine Union and that is true, unconditional Divine Love.

Everything is at peace, in Truth, and soaked in Divine Love.

My friend, "Love is your true nature."

Experience Love! Give Love! Be Love!

Love and Blessings!
Dadashreeji

December, 2016

Before me, many had delivered

teachings and techniques

for your salvation and liberation.

I am not here to repeat them,

but to deliver that experience

in your heart so that it becomes

your own personal Truth.

\- Dadashreeji

Interviews

I am not a mystic or a fortune teller;

neither a saint nor a sage;

I am not a Guru, Master, or God.

Do not categorize me in any of these.

I am just you –

your Higher sacred Self.

- Dadashreeji

A Transforming Presence

How old are you?

I am thirty-four years old. But even if you come to see me twenty years hence, I'll look the same. But you can call me Dadashreeji.

Are you enlightened?

It is difficult to say that because to admit it would mean that I still have the 'I' left in me. I do not possess any sense of the ego in human terms.

Can you explain it further?

Though I can talk to you right now as normally as a person should to another person, my vision is not linear anymore. I can go to any plane of existence, draw my references from there, and speak through it. If the universe is all places between one to hundred, then my consciousness can take me anywhere depending on the necessity of the time. But that has not prevented me from leading the life of an ordinary human being. I have a wife and a young son, and I easily relate with him on his plane of comprehension.

How did this happen to you?

Though I am a medical doctor by profession, I was an atheist.

I was a science-oriented person and doubted the existence of a supreme power at play behind this worldly projection. Yet at the same time, I could not help but marvel at the intelligence that lay behind the faultless design of the human body. In the year 1997, I came across the scripture called Das Bodh written by the Maharashtrian Saint Samarth Ramdas in the 17th century. Das Bodh expounds the themes of discrimination between the true and the untrue, and provides methods on how to function and excel in society from a place of deep spiritual understanding. Reading Das Bodh made me consider the possibility of a Supreme Intelligence, sourcing this unfathomable yet magnificent world.

Inspired, I began to meditate daily. As my meditation increased I gradually began to have visions of saints, historical figures, deities, and eventually of Mahavataar Babaji. Babaji revealed to me my past lives on this earth. He told me about my mission in this life and has constantly been in touch with me ever since to help raise human consciousness.

A doctor's place is considered close to God. Why did it not satisfy you?

While doing internship in a hospital, I was struck by the limitations of a doctor in relieving human suffering. There was this fourteen year-old boy whose father was jailed for burning his wife to death. He was homeless and penniless with three sisters to look after. His aunt gave him some fruits to eat, but he decided to sell them in order to make money for livelihood. Unfortunately, the same day he met with an accident and broke his arm. Inside the hospital his sisters would sleep under his bed as they had nowhere to go. I felt I could heal him only physically, and painfully fell short of the knowledge required to mitigate his emotional and circumstantial suffering. Though I do not practice the medical profession anymore, I am still a doctor. Spiritually, I heal lives completely. I heal the soul.

Why do people suffer?

Human misery is due to karma and the soul's desire to willingly undergo certain hard lessons necessary for its evolution and eventual liberation. Atonement of bad karma can happen in several ways. A person can decide the mode of atonement and willingly undertake a penance. The experience of pain during suffering cleanses the accumulated sins, and deep prayers to God gives relief, provides answers, and removes suffering. Prayer has immense power. Apart from that, virtues like not hurting others, kindness, non-violence, and helpfulness should always be practised to grow spiritually.

Often prayers go unanswered. Why does it happen so?

When people pray or come close to Him, they are stepping from a negative space to a positive one. Due to this all the good karma that they had created in their past and present lives begins to ripen, and people begin to get desired results. But God does not work beyond the laws created by Him. When they have exhausted the good karmas, prayers stop getting answered, and it is a clear sign that they have to shift their consciousness and take it to the next level. Nothing ever happens to people for their downfall. The laws of existence are meant either to support you or to aid you in your growth. A long period of unresponsiveness from God means that the devotee must take his understanding of God to the next level.

• • •

Why are we born?

We are born because the soul willingly takes on a life form that will help it to learn and perfect lessons it had not learnt in previous births. It is purely an act of free will. Though there are other planes which are far better than Earth, with greater life expectancy, yet the learning over there can take thousands of years to complete, whereas on Earth, the karmic repercussions come faster and the evolution too happens faster.

There is much crime on Earth. Do you mean souls decide to be born as criminals? Does crime help in growth?

Negativity exists for the sake of balancing and supporting life. The minimum balance exists in the ratio of 75:25. Even in Satyug where there is 75 per cent goodness, 25 per cent bad shall exist for the sake of balance. Many inferior souls wait for thousands of years to be born and fulfil their lustful desires because Earth has to be supportive of their actions. In today's time, Earth supports the activity of inferior souls because it is dominated by them.

Therefore, if you do bad, you get good results materially these days. But at the same time this is an excellent time to grow spiritually for good souls, even though they exist in small numbers. There are souls who shall not be transformed even if God appears in person before them. That does not mean that the laws of karma do not act on them. The fate of terrorists is a reminder to all of them as to what happens if they carry on with their ways. Still, the possibility of inner transformation can never be ruled out even in their cases. This period, specifically the year 2012, is such a time when many deluded souls can undergo inner transformation and come to the other side. My job is to facilitate this intention of the universe by helping orchestrate that inner shift.

How do you do it?

Most people know about God through their parents, elders, teachers, or religious scriptures. What they have is a belief about God, on the basis of which they try to regulate their lives, whereas God is an experience which has to be felt, tasted, and enjoyed to actually know His real nature. I have not read many scriptures but when Truth was revealed to me I saw scriptures falling way behind in capturing the real essence of God. God is Love and I let people experience that Love and energy in my presence.

But doesn't the presence of a Guru become a hindrance in the path to self-realization? People become attached to the Guru and are loath to move ahead.

As long as the disciple is leaning on the Guru, his learning is incomplete. He is still deluded because he feels that he and the Guru are two separate entities. True transcending of the Guru happens when their consciousness gets merged in each other. When such a stage is reached, the disciple himself leaves and moves ahead to show the path of Truth to others.

You say souls are good or bad, whereas it is believed that people are shades of grey. What is true?

When the soul is in the astral plane it knows clearly whether it is good or lustful. It is the Earth field which is responsible for the shades of grey. The vibrations on Earth are of mixed character. It is difficult for a good person to maintain his purity and for the bad to be completely unaffected by goodness. My guru Mahavataar Babaji had to take me above the Earth's field to impart certain knowledge which was not possible to be shared on the ground.

How can you singlehandedly uplift the consciousness of the masses?

If a single human being is transformed, he acts as a magnet that attracts other eager souls. Apart from that, young men and women associated with me run several programmes like Global Peace Light Services, Youth Force for Better India (now Youth for Global Peace and Transformation), Neopower Waves for professionals (now International Academy of Transformative Leadership), and an NGO called Kalki Tejomaya Social Welfare Trust (now MaitriBodh Charitable Trust) where through selfless service to humanity they not only cleanse their own souls but uplift others as well.

Is there a thing called final liberation?

Yes, there is liberation and there exists a place from where the soul does not have to return. It is not necessarily a place situated somewhere in space. The place from where I am functioning is also the same. Liberation is essentially a state of being.

Life Positive Magazine, September 2012

• • •

Call of the Divine

Tell us something about your early life, where you were born, your family background, former name and places where you grew up.

I was born in Mumbai on 27 December, 1977, and was raised in Mumbai only. My parents were from a middle class family. My father was a lab-technician and my mother was a housewife. Both of them live with me. My parents named me Mangesh.

All this appears now as the story of another lifetime, and I do not relate to it so much. I do not wish to reveal my surname because that would limit my identity to a particular caste. Since childhood I used to feel and think differently from other children of my age. I remember when I was in class IV, I asked a fellow student why there was a difference between him and I? Why is it that he and I did not think alike? Why couldn't I be him and he be I? He was baffled by my questions.

I was a science student and not specifically inclined to know God, although I believed in universal energy through the concepts of Physics. When I entered the 12th standard, changes began to take place. After I joined medical school, the faultless design of the human body made me wonder about the intelligence sourcing this perfection.

Then I happened to read Das Bodh, a treatise written by Saint Samarth Ramdas on the nature of God, nature of illusion, and ways to function in life from a space of deep spiritual understanding. Das Bodh inspired me to meditate. As I meditated I began to have visitations of saints, deities, and historical figures. Finally, Mahavataar Babaji appeared before me and revealed my True Self and life purpose in 2006.

What was that life purpose?

That I was a Divine being. My Divinity and onward path was revealed in stages to me by Mahavataar Babaji. My body too had to evolve to acclimatize to the changes in consciousness. I used to get fever in those times but since I knew what was happening I could bear it. By 2011 things were very clear to me, and He asked me to interact with people.

What do you mean by being a Divine being? Are you God?

What do you understand by God?

God is omnipresent, all-powerful, all-knowing, can hold everything whereas humans are the opposite.

For you that may be the definition of God. For me I am somebody to help and deliver. Divinity is not static...It is an ongoing, ever expanding phenomenon. There is still so much to know and explore.

Is there anybody beyond you?

I don't see anyone beyond me. I do have a Guide called Mahavataar Babaji, but basically He and I are one.

• • •

If you are God, then why did you go through the human experience of illusion? Avataars have been born with full knowledge of their divinity at the time of their birth.

Every incarnation functions as per the purpose of that incarnation and the need of that time. In all my previous incarnations I have functioned from my Highest Self. I could never know what a human being feels when he falls sick, gets rejected, feels hurt, suffers losses, and faces failure. In this incarnation, I wanted to experience the human condition in order to understand it. So I arranged for temporary illusion to cover me, and also for the stage-wise revelation of my true nature through Mahavataar Babaji.

What is your past-life relationship with Mahavataar Babaji?

Mahavataar Babaji has been on Earth since 5,000 years. I met Him in His previous lifetimes once, and we discussed the human evolution and the ways in which Masters can guide. It was agreed that we would share a Master-disciple relationship in this age. Right now, Mahavataar Babaji is guiding through fifty-four people initiated by Him on planet Earth. But His way of functioning through all of them is different and depends on the purpose of that being. Someone is awakening people through Kriya yoga, someone is teaching meditation, someone else is teaching mantras. With me no tools are required. You simply have to be in my presence and you will see the change in yourself.

People claim phenomenal change in themselves after coming in touch with you. How do you do it?

• • •

What does sugar do? It sweetens everything it touches. You cannot ask sugar why it is sweet. Same is with me. It is my nature to boost Divinity in people.

Can you give self-realization to people?

Yes, I can give self-realization.

But Gurus say that it is not possible for anybody to give self-realization to others.

Now they will see it happening over here, with me.

But can anybody reach this stage with you or only those with a certain kind of spiritual history?

Anybody coming to me will see change in himself.

You say that good times are coming and it cannot be prevented. People who have worked for these times earlier have been reborn to taste the fruit of their labor. Can you shed some more light on this?

Previously many good souls, especially those trying hard to work in harmony with divine laws, had the vision of seeing something positive in the world, but because of the time it was not happening. So there was no result for the work they did at that time. Ever since the wheel of time turned in the positive direction, they began to take birth since they were all waiting for this moment. Their birth at this time is to enjoy the benefits of labor they did previously. You will find many such good souls around you.

• • •

You once talked about one world and one religion. Do you agree that so many religions create problem among people?

In this world, fight is only over the concept of religion. My God will Love in my way and your God will Love in your way, and then there is a fight over these issues. In the coming years, all the confusing things which have polluted the scriptures will be wiped out. Only Absolute Truth will remain.

How will it happen? Attachment to outdated religious doctrines appears to be the biggest roadblock to human evolution.

When the sun is down, it is very difficult to see things. When the sun rises, there is no need for artificial lighting. In the same way, when the dark ages are there, it is very difficult to distinguish good from bad, but as the Golden Era enters, all false things get wiped out naturally.

All religions are good. The lack of understanding of religion is causing problem right now, and there is no one who can give proper understanding to people. Ideally in one single life, you should be able to experience all the religions. Then a person should be able to decide which religion he is more in sync with and follow it. It is the communities who have made it a stricture that you cannot change the religion you have been born into. The good things in religion have been altered, and observation of rituals has been made more important than the essence of religion. If a Christian does not read the Bible but relates to Jesus Christ deeply, is he not a Christian? If a Hindu does not practice the essence of Hinduism which is Vasudhaiv Kutumbakam (the world is one family), is he a true Hindu? All the religions should help you to grow from within. Understand religion well. Clear the concepts about religion. Take up one concept of religion and study it well.

Apart from transformation is there any other aim and purpose of the MaitriBodh Parivaar?

Yes. It is the establishment of One World, One Community, and One Truth. When I went to Europe a few months ago, a woman cried copiously when I was departing, saying that I belonged to India and was going back there. I felt bad to see that nationalities have created barriers between people. I belong to the entire human race, to the whole planet. I only happen to be born in India. My entire work is of 200 years. It has been divided into four arms:

1. *Transformation of Self*

2. *Dissolution of ignorance*

3. *Liberation of the individual*

4. *Establishment of Love and Truth.*

It will put good and bad in separate spaces. The good people of all religions will come together on one side.

What is the greatest hurdle in the path of your mission?

The greatest hurdle is the unwillingness of people to change. People want to enjoy divinity but do not want to change. If they do not listen they have to go through the same mistakes which they have done before. And in such cases, I cannot do anything. I have to wait until they are ready to change. I request people to be willing to change. I will take care after that. People are very unaware that speaking ill about anyone is not a spiritual quality. Any person who is worshipping God, but speaking ill about anyone cannot be a true pundit or priest.

What is the future of human race and this planet?

Great. It is going to be a lot of fun. Very bright under the umbrella of the Divine. There would be no separation, no communities, no injustice happening in the world. In that period, everyone would be strongly aware of the presence of Divinity.

The human race crossed Kalyug in the year 2012. People related it with a mystical event which did not happen, but changes did take place and were independent of any mystical happening. Right now we are in the initial phase of Satyug. This Satyug will not be like the Satyug of yore where you had rishis sitting under trees and meditating. The energies would be the same but the manifestation would be different. For example, cars would be there but they would be made in such a way that they do not pollute the environment. Similarly for other technologies. There are some major events which are lined up to take place. They would be revealed to people at the right time. The year 2032 is a good time to witness what I have said. The positivity and the goodness of the times would be in full manifestation.

What do you have to say about the ills of the present time?

The existing system will try very hard to resist being dislodged. The more good energies spread on the planet, the more negative energies become desperate to hold their ground. What you see is a reflection of that struggle. I request everyone to join hands and pray for the suffering humanity. Conditions in Syria and Iraq are very bad. Girls are unable to step out of their homes.

Recently an Indian Guru went there to help them. Do you also plan to go?

I do not need to go there physically to help people. I can do it from here as well, but for that I need prayers. Prayers give me the reason to intervene – the power to act. Otherwise I can only watch. I cannot break the rules I have created myself. If a lawmaker breaks the law then who will uphold it? I urge people to wake up and start taking responsibility for the ills around them. You can no longer ignore the call of the helpless. Today, you may be feeling safe within your homes, thinking that by closing your door you are shutting out the problems, but you never know when they will come knocking at your door as well.

Life Positive Magazine, April 2015

• • •

A Divine Friend

Dadashreeji, who are you?

I am your true friend – someone to just help and guide you, and make your life complete. I am here to help you experience and fulfil the purpose of your life. I realized mine because of my Master, Mahavataar Babaji, who appeared to me in the year 2006 and initiated me as His disciple. He has been working to help many spiritual beings on this planet Earth to help them experience the reality. He has been serving mankind since many many years. For me, He is a true Friend, He is true Love.

When I see Him now, I don't see any separation between Him and I; it is as if we are One. So I do not see a separate Mahavataar Babaji; for me it is like the two sides of the same coin. And what connects us is the Love, which is the ultimate reality that we all experience.

How did it happen to you when you went from being a medical doctor to a spiritual guide?

Since childhood, I wanted to help people and take them out of their sufferings. That motivated me to become a doctor. But when I joined my medical practices later, I realized that I had my limitations – limitations to help people at the physical level. So that was when my journey started – to look for a solution to end the sufferings of people, which is not only physical, but psychological, emotional, and spiritual. So I would say that I am still a doctor, but rather than a medical doctor, I'am a spiritual doctor to help people realize the cause of their suffering. This has taken me further on this path where now I am able to guide people and help them come out of their suffering and experience the Truth of life.

Many people seek a spiritual Master to tell them what to do or how to solve their problems. What would you answer them?

When you are feeling sick, you visit a doctor. Suppose, you and your friend are both sick and visit the same doctor together. It may be possible that you have a headache and your friend has a stomach ache. Will the doctor prescribe the same medicine for both of you? That wouldn't happen. The doctor would try to know the history, the problem behind your complaints, and accordingly advise you the prescription. Likewise, there cannot be the same spiritual remedy or a treatment for everyone. So I would not, or we do not, recommend only one way to help everyone. There cannot be a single treatment for all the diseases or issues people have physically or psychologically.

However, at the same time, what I can advise is a change in your thinking pattern, a change in your lifestyle. The best way that you can have, as a human being, is to be a student, a student in life. Wherever you go, whatever you do, in the way you think and act, see yourself as a student of life. The entire life of yours is a school and you are here to learn. Everyone who comes across you – your friends, relatives, in fact, everyone

• • •

associated with you – are there to help you grow, to teach you something to help you move ahead in life. So be a student in your life!

The second thing which I can advise you is to keep moving in life, to keep working. Do not stop anywhere! Whatever you are doing, your duty has to be for yourself and all the people associated with you. So keep moving and keep working!

And the third, last thing that I can say is – share goodness. Anything good which you have, share it with others. These are three very simple things. But if you just practice them, you will see for yourself how things will change for you. You will be able to witness the transformation and move towards the reality of your life; slowly, steadily, but for sure.

Couple, family, friendship – what is the main ingredient to keep relationships in harmony?

Every relation that you have in your life – as friend or parents, brothers-sisters – all these relations are there to complete you, to make you understand who you are in this world and what is the purpose of your coming. Sometimes in these relationships, we see conflicts; there may be misunderstanding or arguments. We may also come across unhealthy relations with people amongst us, most likely with close relations, people who are very near to us.

There are two things that I can suggest for you all which you should look forward to in your relations. The first is patience – patience from your side; and the second is understanding – understanding within the relationship. Patience will come only if you have Love within. Patience comes out of Love, and understanding comes out of an open communication. Love is something which you can't try; you can't practice to Love someone. Love has to happen! So you have to wait for that. But communication is something which you can practice. So any relation can be healed when you have open communication with the people around, especially with your near and dear ones. And when you have understanding in your relationship, Love will automatically flow, and that will complete your relation with people.

There comes a time in life when you feel lost and with no way out....How will you know the next step to take?

Imagine that you are driving a car and you reach a roundabout or a traffic circle. What happens when you reach the circle? You reach a point where there are too many roads, too many directions – right, left, and then straight. So what to do when you reach there? You may think that there is nowhere to go ahead; you may think 'I am lost'. But to be very clear, there are many ways to go ahead. It is not that you are lost somewhere, but rather like you are confused with life at that point of time and you see no directions to go ahead. So what you have to do is wait and find the right path to move ahead.

In life, whenever you experience that state of confusion – that there is no path to go ahead – know that it comes only when there is a possibility of a change in your life. Whenever you experience this 'I have lost myself' or 'there is no path to go ahead' feeling, or you're confused to take decisions, it means it is time for a change. It is time for you to look forward to the opportunities which are there in front of you. So, I would say that there is no situation in which you are lost; maybe you have just stopped looking for a different way in your life. But there are always ways, paths for you still which are inviting you to go ahead. So, what is important for you at that point is to decide – to decide which path to select, which path to take, and then move on ahead.

Will the planet Earth live an era of global peace? How to achieve that?

Yes, it is possible for all of you to experience that Peace Era. In fact, I'am very very sure at this period of time. Maybe it was difficult in the previous ages, but now it is very sure that people are going to experience this Peace Era. When you are moving ahead in this life with that intention – that I'am looking for that change, I am looking towards that harmonized world all around – you will see that happening. You will witness that happening in this very life. The good sign for all of us to see is that many people across the world have started longing for a change. And, this change is not only within; people want that change even in the world outside. Both of this is going to take you towards experiencing that Peace Era. The Peace Era will not happen unless you want it, unless you really need it. The good point is that you need it. Hence, it is going to happen for you all.

Religions have taught us that suffering is a way to grow in consciousness. Do we really need to go through the pain or can we evolve even in joy?

Definitely not. You do not have to suffer all the time to experience the reality of your life. What is important is as you said rightly – do we evolve? I would say, we always evolve.

Anything that happens, whatever happens, we always evolve within. We always grow in consciousness, irrespective of pain or happiness. Right now, when we are talking to each other, I suppose you are not suffering, you are not crying as we interact with each other. But there is a change in you. You are able to experience that evolution within, you are able to see that – yes, there is some shift happening within us. So every moment of our life, we learn something; every moment we are growing in consciousness.

Maybe people think suffering is necessary because many people in this world are suffering as of now. So, maybe this is a cry – the emotional cry or a spiritual cry from people that maybe because people are suffering, so you have to suffer to experience the spiritual reality of life. But the fact is – it is not so. The entire process of evolution is about your inner Self and your mind. That's all! So what happens after that is your internal story. It has nothing to do with your pain, suffering , or happiness. It is just moving ahead, just learning through the lessons of life, and you will see that you are growing in consciousness.

Interview in Milan, 2015

• • •

Christmas Special

I often visit different regions and different places and interact with the people. I have found that the human mind is the same. It doesn't change much. The differences that we usually encounter are the cultural differences – the way the day begins and what one does in the daily activities. However, the human mind is the same, and the main functioning of spirituality is dealing with your mind. The good part which I see is that people are very receptive for a change towards life through spirituality, and that is a very promising sign for the entire world. A lot of great changes, positive changes would happen through the European region.

Can you make yourself spiritually at home in the so-called eternal city of Rome – the center of the Christian world?

Oh yes! Definitely, it is like being at home. Being here for the last two-three days has been great. It has been great because one can experience the beginning of a religion here – the religion of Love. I won't specifically call it Christianity, but Love. And I could feel it so profoundly, so powerfully here in

Rome. It's been a great honour for me to be a part of this great city.

In December, Christianity celebrates incarnation and birth of Jesus Christ. How do you relate to Christmas?

Christmas is a celebration of life. It's to commemorate someone who can be seen as ideal, someone who has really sacrificed his life for Love. And, there cannot be a better day than Christmas when you experience that Love in your life. And, Love is what you have to share with each and everyone around. You cannot celebrate Christmas by being alone in your house and closing the doors and windows and sitting by the candlelight all alone. Christmas means being out with people. That's what the quality of Love is – to get together with everyone around and make them part of your Love, make them part of your own existence in this world. That's the purpose of Christmas I look forward to.

So, it's basically about sharing?

Yes, sharing Love.

If a student in your Ashram in Karjat near Mumbai asked you who Jesus is, what would your answer be?

People have asked me this question. Many people, especially those who come from Europe to attend the sessions, have this curiosity to know who Jesus is. For me, Jesus is my true Friend, and what connects me with Jesus is pure Love. He has been someone who has really set a milestone for many people – those who are beginning their spiritual path or those who just want to help people. He is someone that you can look towards as the Highest, someone who has been able to transform people through Love. And, for all of us in India, Jesus is like the Love Incarnate – someone who suffered a lot in his life just to convey the message of Love, which is next to impossible for any human being to do.

It was for the sake of humanity that He had to go through all that suffering – for the ills and the wrongdoings that happened at that time. The time was such that the worst could have happened and people could have gone through really critical situations, but by taking all the suffering upon Himself, He averted the same.

He was someone, in fact, the only one, who could withhold or bear all that pain; and He went through with it. He knew about everything that was going to happen to Him, and still He went through with it. He experienced that pain only to liberate, only to relieve people's pain for that period of time. He knew the future of Christianity, and that His path was going to liberate so many people. Such a being is rare, and we see Him as one of the highest Love Incarnate of that time.

The first message would always be the same – be Love, experience Love within. And, the second message would be – celebrate life, celebrate life now. There are going to be very nice positive moments from here onwards for the entire humanity. And for that, you all need to move forward and celebrate this life. And you have Christmas, which is the best day that you have each year to celebrate life with Love. In fact, you should celebrate life so that everyday becomes your Christmas.

The Catholic Church prays in the service to await Jesus' return. Will He?

Oh yes. Definitely. You would see that.

When will we see that?

When you see that, you will know it. So I would definitely not predict it now. But He is working a lot for the humanity and very soon people will experience His physical manifestation. And, I would say, as of now, leave it to the time for people to experience. Because even if I tell you now, it will be like a story from a book which you have read or a fantasy. There are few things which people need to witness.

Are you really talking about physical manifestation like 2000 years ago or…?

You will see that happening very soon, and it will be only to guide people from here onwards.

Why is there so much harm and misery in the world?

You notice that very soon it's going to be nightfall – sometime after 9 or 10 o'clock. There will be darkness everywhere and you wouldn't go out. So, your operations would be within the walls of this house. If we switch off the light here as well, then it's going to be dark in here too. When there is no light at all and it's all dark that is when all the ills, all the wrongdoings will take place. So, what you are pointing out is exactly what is happening when people are experiencing the darkness in their life.

If you want to come out of it, then just wait for the day, which will surely come. Then you can open the window, and the doors. You can go out and see God; see His Light and the suffering will just vanish. But, people want to stay inside the house, people want to just lock the door and the windows and remain in that darkness. So, when you are in the darkness, you are going to suffer. All you have to do is just come out of the house and you will see a change.

What is your assessment towards our future? Do you believe that goodness will prevail?

Yes. 100%. I'am very very sure about it because the good sign is many people are changing. Many people all around the world are changing or they are looking forward to a change. The good part is that it is not only a change within, but also in the outside world, and people are calling for that change. It's not necessary they have to follow a religion or a God, but they are feeling for a change – yearning for something positive to happen all around. And, people are responding well towards it. That should be a sign for all of you to know that there is something good going to happen. And from my side, I can assure you for sure that a very good, positive, and peaceful time and a harmonious world that all of you would be able to see is round the corner. You would see all of these in this life itself; you don't have to wait for some ages to pass.

• • •

So, the level of consciousness has gone up?

Yes, it has. And people are witnessing it.

There are people who say that it is possible to remember the future. 5,000 years ago, the Indian rishis are said to have written down the destiny of human race and many individuals on palm leaves. The predictions really occurred. So, has the future already happened?

Everything that you can see happening in the world, especially the predictions which you are mentioning here, depends on the calculations on how a person is going to go ahead in his life and how many births he would take. So, based on the calculations, it has all been predicted by someone 5,000 years back.

But at the same time, I want to clarify here that not everything is predestined. Not everything which you see is going to happen for sure. If you go to visit any palmist or astrologer, he would be able to predict only a part of your life, not everything. That would be a major part of your life – the marriage, the children, brother-sisters, and job – but not friends, not what is going to happen today and every day. Because only 20% of your life can be predicted, not more than that. There is something called free will, which keeps changing. So, predictions are true to a certain extent, but not for 100% of your life.

What we see in front of our eyes, is that reality?

If you look at it in one way, for some people, it is reality. Because they sense, they feel, they can touch, they can smell, for them it is reality. However, for someone who is awakened, it is a false world. It's going to disappear very soon when you leave your body. For the awakened person, it's just an illusion, just a dream.

But if you think everything around you is real, then for you it becomes reality. If I pinch you, you will feel it, there is something happening there. But in reality, if you see the universal reality, it's just a dream passing by – phase by phase. You are there just to witness and play your own part in that.

So, each and every person does have a special part?

Yes, 100%. Let's take the example of a football game. Suppose, there are players playing on the ground. You can't say any particular player in the team has no role. Every player has his own role and is doing something for the team to win.

The same is the case for you and everyone here. Anyone who is taking birth on this planet has some role. If at this moment, you are living, breathing, or are able to walk as a human being, it means that Nature wants you to live in this world. It means that you have a purpose to live.

How can we remember the purpose?

Every human being has a sub conscious mind. When you go within yourself, you may be able to reach the sub conscious mind. If that is the case, then it might pass a message to you about the purpose of your life. Otherwise, a Divine awakening is required, when the voice within comes out so strongly and tells you what you are supposed to do in your life. That would be very easy then.

• • •

177

But if you are not able to understand the purpose of your life, what option do you have? Whatever you are doing now, anything that you have in your hand today, at this period of time, just do it best! Give your 100% and do justice to it. And that's it! Don't look for anything beyond it.

Do time and space exist?

Yes. When there is space, there would be time. When you experience from within that there is no space, then there is no time. And, when you are awakened into that state, altered state of consciousness, you reach a point where there is no space. The moment that you see there is no space, there is no time for you to travel. Then, you are everywhere at that period of time.

Are we dreamers or are we being dreamt by God?

Both. You are dreaming and, yes, someone is dreaming about you too. So when you leave your body, when you come out of a dream, then you become part of that consciousness which is dreaming all this. It is just like when you sleep at night, you are dreaming, but you are there in your dream also. So both are real – you are dreaming, and you are a part of your dream.

And this would mean that we would have to wake up from the dream?

Yes. And that's very easy. Just connect with the Divine and it will just happen.

What happens after a human death?

There is a journey. You see a human being as the ultimate form

• • •

of evolution, but it just plays a part for the journey of the soul. You learn something, you grow and then your growth continues ahead after the death. Now this is an idea that people may or may not believe in; but the Truth does not change. When you leave your body, you will have more clarity about this journey. This is an ongoing journey which never ends until you reach the Light. When you reach the Light, then you just merge yourself there, and enjoy the association of the Highest Light.

You are so clear and so precise in your response, who are You?

I am your friend, a true Friend. If the human mind is going to ask me, then I am a very good Friend of yours. And, if the spiritual seeker is going to ask me, then my answer is – I'am your guide; I can guide you well in your life. And, if it is ego, then I'am the best person to kill your ego.

I have read that Mahavataar Babaji appeared in front of you in 2006. Would you please describe this experience?

Yes, sure. I was always in the process of knowing more about life since childhood. As a child I would ask questions like – "Why is there a difference between you and me?" or "What separates your consciousness and my consciousness?" I had been looking for answers for many many years when I was in school.

The journey went on for many years and I happened to become a medical doctor as I wanted to help people and heal them well. The same profession led me to know more about the Truth of existence. And, I started working on myself – through meditations or many other things which I could do from my side.

And in 2006, Babaji appeared before me. At that point of time, I was not very clear about who He was. He initiated me as His disciple according to a ritual, which is done by a Master for a disciple. At that time, I had no idea because I was not someone who followed the culture or rituals. For me it was a completely new experience, and then, at the end of the process, He told me, "I declare you as my disciple, and now you have to go ahead and guide people."

My life changed after that, everything changed. Babaji also revealed to me what lay ahead in the future, year by year, year by year. A time came, when I came to know Who I am. I knew for what purpose I have come here. And since then, the journey has been going so well, the mission has been spreading so well, so effectively.

Can you give self-realization?

Yes. Yes, sure definitely.

In which way?

My method of operating on people is through Grace. Grace is the only way for me that I can function through. So when I am talking to you at the same time, I'm operating through Grace. The mind will not be able to know or comprehend what's happening, but the heart knows it. The heart would feel something happening, that there is something which is happening. So I work through Grace, which deals with your heart and the core of your existence.

• • •

Are we all one with universal energy?

Yes, we are one. So when you experience yourself – that you are a human mind – immediately your next experience is separation from the universal consciousness. The moment your mind shifts and gets dissolved into the real consciousness of your being, you experience oneness with the entire universal consciousness. For instance, when Babaji acts in the physical body, He is separate from me and Jesus in the physical body. But within, we all experience we are one. We operate through different bodies, and through different qualities we express ourselves. But it is the same universal consciousness, it's the Divine consciousness that we operate from.

So you are all brothers and sisters?

Yes. But rather than looking at it as brothers and sisters, it is as friends. We are all friends.

What are your aims and goals for the MaitriBodh Parivaar?

As I told you now – as friends. We are all friends. We are just looking forward to making a family of friends. The family of ten-fifteen-twenty-hundreds-thousands – all connected by a bond of friendship. If we find this family everywhere, all over the globe, what remains at the end is the One World, One Community, One Truth.

There would be no fight because of religion or region or country or race. We would all be a part of the same family. So what is up there – at the Divine plane of existence – will be reflected back onto this Earth. And where you all, as a family, need to experience as One. That's the initiative we have begun.

• • •

And you will see that happening effectively – year by year, year by year. There would be no separations because of a religion, there would be no separations because of a region, and all would be experiencing as One within, as one family, bonded together with true Love.

Interview in Rome, 2015, with Susan Stahnke

• • •

An Evening with Dadashreeji

Times are changing. Transformation has started. You have to flow with it. You don't have to do much about it. Only option that you have is to flow with this time, and it's going to be more and more intense for all of us as we flow together as a part of the society. We are playing our role to convey to all our friends, loved ones, close ones to be a part of this journey.

The best that we can offer is to help you reach that state of freedom, peace, and Love within, but it's very important for you to know where you stand today. Is it material achievement, or success, or is name and fame everything for you? If we see the journey of our lives, we happen to go through similar sequences. All of us, our stories are almost the same. Some people do it very well, some people take time. Is it entirely by your efforts or your luck or by the Grace of God? What is exactly happening and where are we today? When I observed this, I saw that there are three phases of life that one can encounter or be in.

I. SELF-CONFINEMENT

Somehow we stop our growth. Growth according to us does

not mean money, name, or fame. It is an internal state. How do you feel about yourself within? Self-confinement means that there is a question within you – What shall I do in my life today? What is there for me to do?

And this state happens only when you reach a position where there is no way out to move ahead, to go ahead. It's almost a dead end in your life. Somehow we get cornered and we seek for guidance and help. So help may arrive from friends, relatives, or maybe internally, you feel like doing something about it. But many people are somehow unable to come out of this phase and unable to make themselves better.

So two things may happen:

1. *You start withdrawing yourself from everything you do – not meeting people, avoiding family functions, and not interacting with people. Somehow you start complaining about everything in your life. And this is what I was talking about – confining your own growth, confining your True Self.*

2. *You start dominating others. It's surprising but people do behave like this to cover up their own blockages, their own weaknesses. They somehow try to dominate others. These people normally speak very loudly, but internally they are somehow confined. They start complaining about everything in the world. If such a person happens to be your friend or a close colleague, and he is yelling at you, scolding you, or insulting you, understand this that he is asking for help from you. So he is not blaming you or judging you as wrong. He is saying that he needs help. Will you help him?*

From next time be aware of this and please be there as a good awakened being. Help those people.

Either of this may happen. Either you withdraw yourself or start dominating others. Mainly those people who have no option but to socialize with others and interact with people but have no time to go within and see their internal state, behave in this way. They have to project themselves in a different way. But I would like you to know that you check yourself as well at the same time.

I see this confined state as a very good state because there is an opportunity for you to grow because you are looking forward to do something in your life. You seek guidance. You seek help. If this state remains untreated for long, that is not something which is ideal. You have to do something about it. So many times, we tell people that it's very important that you act immediately. Don't wait for something to happen. If you feel internally like doing something, please immediately act towards it.

II. UNCERTAINTY

In this, many people have achieved a lot of material things. They maybe famous and successful people, but even at that path they feel they have a question within – Is it really something which I was supposed to do? Was this planned for me? Or was I supposed to do something different? Is this the path for me? Is this work for me?

Someone is a very good and renowned doctor but he still has a pain in his heart and it says – "I wanted to be a good

• • •

singer. I wish I could have joined three-four years back. I would have enjoyed this life in a much better way." This is uncertainty – what I am doing today is something I shouldn't do or I should have done something better than this.

And know this well, understand this well, that you have only one life. How many days are left, we don't know. How many months are left, we don't know. So it's really important that you do what you really wanted to do. Today we are going to not just talk about problems or issues, but also come to solutions.

Coincidentally, I happen to be a medical doctor so my job is to first understand problems, issues, illnesses, and then we can go forward to treat it well – that's how my natural approach is. I hope it's fine with you all because I haven't studied any spiritual books, Vedas, or scriptures. I do believe in all that but I haven't gone through those. What I can do is help you get transformed internally and that happens without any talk, without any interaction; you can still feel it. We are sharing very important factors of human life – what is it that I can do today, now, for my life?

One of the best friends of every human being today on this planet is G for Google. For any question, you take your smart phone and Google it. I don't know how good it is but Google is your friend, and I would like to replace that with proper Guidance in life. Because whatever we are sharing today maybe just very simple, easily available information in any of the books that you read or must have heard somewhere, but the difference here is that you will experience it, within yourself. You will know it for sure and there's no confusion

• • •

after that. If it is A then it is A, if it is B then it is B. You will all get that much clarity. Without analyzing it, without digging much deeper into it, you would just know it automatically within.

When you are sitting over here, even if you don't understand whatever was told to you here, it's all right. This is exactly what happens in our Ashram. People just come and rest but when they go back, they experience that shift within, they experience that something has happened. Mind fails to understand what that was but that's how it is. I want you to take a step ahead in your life – that's the only intention that we have. It is only about your growth, your individual growth. It is not about religion or community or cult – but just a help by a friend to another friend, a very honest effort. So whatever we are going to give you here or offer you is only and only for your growth. We will talk about the current issues, the current state of human mind, and you can shape your life accordingly.

It's good for those people who know about their purpose of life and I'm sure they must be doing really good. But we are talking about those who somehow couldn't reach it. Just because someone else was doing it, he or she did it. Just because the parents had it so he or she is also having it. What is it exactly that you want to do in your life? This phase of uncertainty, I would say, is not good as compared to self-confinement because in this state you are doing something that you don't want to, and that causes more trouble, more frustration and irritation within. It's better not to do that and wait for something that you really want to do here onwards.

III. FULFILLMENT

It happens for those people who have achieved what they wanted to. It is for those who aimed for bigger dreams, for those who knew their purpose in life. They work towards it, they achieve it, and today they are successful people. Having said this, even they have a question and the question is – "Am I missing something in my life? I got everything that I wanted. I have done everything. People respect me. I have earned a lot of money. People see me as a successful person but still I am missing something in my life."

And this is a very very good state. It's a very good phase. In fact, here onwards you start exploring yourself. You start exploring Truth. You take a step towards something which is right, and then you seek for guidance for help. Your approach towards life changes. It is less practical and more humanly-based on your emotions, based on your Truth of life. What you receive afterwards is all positive in abundance, absolute fullness within, experiencing that completeness. We want to help all those and guide all those who happen to be a part of this.

When I experienced this (because I have gone through all these different phases) and when I encountered the last phase of fulfillment, I saw that shift within – a human mind changing into an all together different Divine mind which is free of all conditions, fears, inhibitions within, and resistance. Everything which was unwanted was replaced with Love and care. And, I hope all of us together make it in this life only. In fact, not hope, I would say, all of you should experience this.

This journey is an internal and personal journey. It's not for people to declare. It's not a public proclamation that you

• • •

have gone spiritual, or that you follow a certain organization or a Master, or that your preferences of life have now changed. It is not like that; it is entirely personal and internal. It's your internal world that you deal with. It has nothing to do with the outside world, and this is where we want to help you out. If you are finding a purpose of life, we can help you to go closer to it.

****

What is it that you should do today if we erase everything of your past? There is no identity at all, no recognition. Forget whatever has happened till now. Today is the first day or the first moment of your life. Hereon, a new life is given to you. For a while forget your name, forget your identity. No fame, no name, nothing absolutely associated with your identity.

What is it that one should do? Begin this life again from that zero. Isn't it good to have that opportunity to restart a life? Every day you get this opportunity to restart your life but somehow you forget it. That moment was there today also. Do you know what was that moment? That is when you get up early in the morning every day. In your deep sleep, somehow you come out of your material identity as if there is absolutely nothing and when you get up in the morning, you start regaining your name, your status, your people, your family, and then you act accordingly. So every day you are getting this opportunity to restart your life. But what do you do? You repeat what was there yesterday. Again you follow the same sequence. And then you say, "Why does nobody like me ? Why does nobody Love me? I do good. People do bad to me." All those things get repeated again and again. But today again this opportunity is given to you to restart. What is the first thing that you can do?

Define your personal goal. For a while take out everything – your name, your job, your money. What is it exactly that your heart wants to do? Sometimes you're afraid of coming out of that comfort zone.

To be very honest with you and to make you understand – here onwards, as times are going to change, everyone is going to be challenged by the situation around – natural changes, people around, family, society. Everything is going to change and things are going to challenge you anyhow. Even if you don't respond to this or don't act with this, the situations are going to change. You are not completely a separate individual. You are a part of the society. Society itself is changing so you will also. So as an individual, talk to your heart. Today is a good opportunity for you to talk to yourself and ask a question – what do you really want? Any answer may come. And I would appreciate if an illogical answer comes, something which is not practical, because if it is practical that means it is out of your mind. It has to be from your heart. I see anything which is logical is limited because mind has a limitation and we talk about something beyond that which is more profound, more powerful.

So your first duty becomes to work towards that personal dream or personal aim of life, and this will happen to all of you. A thought would come, a voice would come from within, and that will tell you that do this in your life and there will be a positive response.

Second thing which all of you can plan to work towards are your immediate duties, and these are your duties towards your family members and your loved ones. Think something for them that you feel you want to give to all your close people before you leave this earth. Think of something that you'll make sure you give to all your close people – one, two, or three people. Just think for these very close people, loved ones. In what way would you feel satisfied by offering something for them? I am sure it wouldn't be so difficult to do something for them. And, please don't always count help as money – that you will keep some money, bank balance, or properties and the like. This is not going to give security in future. There is much more than that. So, for that what you can do is achieve the best in life and give that best to your people. This is how you can help. This is the second thing.

Thirdly, think of something for the society or any community that you feel connected with – any group, any section of society. Do something for them. Whatever appeals to you. Wherever you feel natural and connected with.

Only three purpose or goals of life one should plan. And you know and I know that none of you will repent after this. Basic, foremost, the most essential things, in anyone's life are these three things. And what we do is, apart from these three things, we look for everything. We gossip, we complain, we blame, we talk about what's happening in someone else's life but we don't focus on these three points, and today is the opportunity for all of you. Even if you understand what I have said now it is more than enough because this message will automatically follow all of you. Nothing in your life, apart from these three goals, should deviate your mind. Whatever happens, any good or bad, your complete focus should be on these points and see afterwards how everything changes so positively. It's not only you who will experience happiness, joy, but others associated with you also will experience it. I have been always serious about my life. I took time to understand everything but I feel I could move a little faster and experience the other side of life. Other side of life means that which is not completely governed or influenced by the human mind.

The current times are very crucial for everyone. Be it a part of this country or any other country, any community, any religion. Everyone has to find their own path and move ahead. All those obstacles, hurdles would be removed if you are ready to go further. Do you feel that these three points are difficult to achieve if you really focus on them or impossible or it's not going to happen at all? This is what, at the end, every human mind is seeking for.

Apart from this, what is it that one should possess, practice, or carry as a quality within to move ahead and experience that Higher Truth, Absolute Truth? What is it which is lacking in all other people when it comes to talking about Truth, Love, bonding?

I have seen people are slowly moving away from it. People have become more practical, more rational, more logical, and success of life is somehow defined by those terms. We would like to change that understanding again. The real life is about emotions. Real life is about caring. Real life is about Love – Love between each and everyone sitting over here or people outside in the world. In what way can you experience it or go towards it?

****

• • •

If the question arises that what shall we do to lead a happy, peaceful, harmonious life, a prosperous life, a successful life wherein I am happy and people with me are also happy?

The first thing that we always suggest and tell people is to **connect to your inner voice**. *Through all those phases which we have covered, all difficult situations, critical times only one thing which helps you is your inner voice. Connecting to your inner voice is the solution. Keep talking to yourself. You see, many a times, you must have experienced or sensed it, even as intuition or insight, that let us do this or this is good for you. And when you followed, you got the result of that so as compared to other person's guidance and inner voice, your own inner voice is always better and higher. And we are here to help you to connect to your own inner voice. Inner voice maybe of any form, of any dimension, any size, or any shape, but it's very important that you connect to your inner voice. We are not talking about God, we are just talking about your own inner Self. Just connect to it. The best thing that you can do for your life, for yourself, is to connect to your inner voice. Even if you forget to do anything else, it's all fine. To be very clear here, even if you lose your money, your identity, your name, and everything else, it's all okay till your connection with inner voice is strong and intact all the time. The moment you see that there is a connection lost – a disconnection between your being and inner voice – somehow you start experiencing that pain, suffering, lack of energy, lack of guidance, and no direction to move ahead. Sincerely, we would like to request all of you to connect to your inner voice. That's the best thing that one can do.*

*Second thing which you can do, which is supposed to be easy but one may find difficult, is to just say thanks to people around – **gratitude**. It's easy but difficult. Saying thanks, conveying thanks has become so difficult. Can we say thanks today for this time?*

Nothing bad happens in life. Everything was good. Everything was positive since the beginning. It was just your mind who judged it as wrong. And I have seen people keep complaining about everything in life and that's not going to help at all. Saying "Thanks!" gives you a more appreciative state of mind, a good sense of feeling so good about yourself. And, when you say thanks to the opposite person, what does he feel? Does he feel like fighting with you or quarreling? No. How do people react normally when you say thanks to someone? He feels good about it. See, if anyone is going to feel good about it, why not do it? Because everyone is doing good or bad for you so appreciate it and say thanks for both of that. You are sensitive people, awakened beings. Only point out positive things and not the negative things. This is very very important.

*So we have understood – connect to inner voice and second is gratitude and the third is to **learn** – learn from your mistake and this part is going to be so so so important from here onwards. Life is going to test everyone and you have no option but to learn from your mistake. Don't repeat your mistake again and again. I am not going to ask what we have done as a mistake, but we need to correct it and this is high time now. We can't postpone it. We can't avoid it. We have to accept it. Now accepting this mistake is not in a way that you call up that person and say, "Oh, I made a mistake!" I am not* *telling you to socially or even to verbally accept it. I am telling you that you accept this mistake within yourself – entirely personal and internal, confidential. You may have a fake smile on your face, which is absolutely fine, but internally accept it once. And, you wouldn't believe the way Nature is going to respond to this. You'll get everything, so positively rewarded. Opportunities and breakthroughs will come. Relationships will be so much better. You will see healthy relationships in your life. We just want you to accept it internally. Nothing more than that. Is it difficult? Anywhere, whatever has happened in your life, just accept it, and that really changes everything; mainly, your approach.*

I remember one day in my life (I vaguely remember a few things of my life) when I was working as an intern doctor in one of the hospitals. There is a casualty duty wherein you have to sit there for twenty-four hours – morning nine to next day morning nine. So it's a twenty-four hours duty and you have one colleague who sits with you. At that time, I used to travel by train, so I somehow reached late at 9:30 a.m. while I was supposed to be there by 9 a.m. So by the time I reached the OPD, my friend who was supposed to be accompanying me was already there. He said, "The chief medical officer is very angry with us, because I also came fifteen minutes late. He scolded me very badly and threatened that he is going to report this to our college." He continued, "Please, go and see him. Just stand and don't say anything. He is very very angry."

And then I realized my mistake in coming late. I missed one train and, as you know, in Mumbai when you miss a train, you get the next one only after ten minutes. So, I came late and realized that the patients suffered, the doctor had gotten angry, and my colleague was taking care of other patients all alone. So there, at that moment, I internally accepted my mistake and resolved to not get late from then onwards, and in case, I got late, then to inform others about it. This was the lesson which I learnt there and then immediately. I learnt it within myself and then I went straight into the cabin of the CMO. I asked him, "Sir, did you call me?" I looked at him knowing that I will accept the mistake. I was ready to answer if he added more into it. He just looked into my eyes and said, "Okay. Go." Nothing more than that.

So, the point in sharing this story with you is that nothing happened afterwards because I accepted internally that: "Yes, this was my mistake." If I would have acted smart and given him some excuse then things would have been a little different that time. I accepted it as it is. It is a very basic act. If you practice it in your life, you will see a change with it. Internally accept it. It's difficult to tell other people so internally accepting would give you a freedom to live in this life. Can we do this internally? Today maybe you can internally go and rest and there you can accept that part of life, even one part where you feel that there is where you went wrong and accept entirely within yourself that that was your mistake, and if you get an opportunity again in future, you would do that same thing in a better way.

These are simple facts of life. When I learnt all these lessons in my life, just through observation, when I was seeking, as a spiritual being, to know about different Truth or higher states of consciousness, what I found at the end is that life is very simple. It's not at all complex. Your mind makes it so, and we want all to live this life happily with simplicity, with no more titles for that. Just flow with it, with no conditions. For me, it's really a beautiful, spiritual, Divine life. For others, it may not be, but we want you to taste it, to experience it, and you can ask for that internally today anytime – that let me experience that side of life which is far beyond this wordly understanding, these worldly conditions.

Today with this given time, I gave what I had to convey, and these teachings and points are specifically directed towards the coming future. After a few months, you would start recollecting all this automatically and then you will know what the importance of this session was. We, as a team, would support you to grow internally, mainly and overall in your life, to go ahead. All masters, all Divine beings, entire Divine consciousness wants people to grow and experience the real side of life, the Truth. And personally, I really enjoyed coming over here because this session was mainly for you all. We are committed to help you, to guide you all, without any conditions, without any expectations. You can experiment on this.

Q&A

Seeker: It seems so simple, but why is it that we cannot take the next step?

Dadashreeji: *Life had been always very simple. Even simpler than the word simple. It's your mind that is playing with you all the time – the tricks of mind, the game of mind, and this mind is influenced because of worldly dimensions, right from your birth till now. For you, the world appears real and then you are so involved in that, you hardly get the opportunity to experience the other side of mind. The nature of human is such that one learns a mistake only by making a mistake, so it takes a lot of time for people to go through it, but it's the layer of your mind which doesn't allow you to the see the other side of life, and that's what takes out the simplicity, so the moment you move towards the core, internal Self of yours, you become more and more simple automatically. So, as we said, connect to your own inner voice. It would make you simpler. So if anyone is mentally very complex that means he is more into logical understanding of world, and when you move away from it, then you become very well an awakened being, a part of society where you sense everyone, you feel for everyone, you care for everyone, and the life changes automatically.*

• • •

Seeker: If there is someone who is seeking help from you but at that moment he is so out of sorts that even though you feel compassion and want to help him, he is not receiving help, how do you give it to him?

Dadashreeji: *If you find any person who is expressing pain or is just scolding and yelling every time or is dominating, in fact, he doesn't give you opportunity to interact with him or even to talk to him, then what he is looking forward, first, is to express all that pain completely, so allow him to do it. So, your duty becomes initially to be there as a listener. Just keep listening to him. All the personal comments at you, don't see them as if he is judging you there. See that he is just expressing his pain. So, as and when he keeps expressing, a point of time will come where he would stop doing it and then he would tell you what he expects from you and that he wants you to take care of him. He wants you to guide him. He wants you to hold his hand and take him forward. All those things he will accept and tell you verbally and then life will change in a better way, but initially he has to empty himself from all that pain. So give him an opportunity, things will change. As well internally also, you can still pray for that person. Externally you just listen, internally you pray for him, and that gives very positive vibes and gives an opportunity for him to be a better person.*

Seeker: Doctors say that people who are aggressive and who keep shouting and screaming all the time suffer from bipolar disorder, so is this a chemical imbalance in the brain or is this an emotional upheaval?

• • •

Dadashreeji: *What causes any chemical imbalance that happens in the brain? What is the cause for it? When I started my journey as a doctor, I was treating only the physical side of pain, and then it became the mental cause behind that pain, so I could see psychosomatic disorders. This mind and the physical body are inter-related, but as and when, I felt like moving ahead and seeing a cause beyond mind, then I could see the emotional turmoil, I could see a spiritual cause behind it, and I felt that if I could treat this everything else was going to get treated. So now, the chemical imbalance has a cause behind it which we see as some emotional imbalance that is further causing some biological imbalance in that person.*

If you consider even this bipolar disorder or if you refer to a psychiatrist's book or any such book of disorders, every mental condition of every person would be described as a disorder or suffering from some disorder. But this is from that book, which relates to it as a disorder. Spiritually, we don't see anyone as suffering from a mental disorder. Everything is internally complex and you have to treat that cause, with that everything will be all right. And, we have seen people changing over here. They accept the fact and they flow accordingly with it. So, I see the cause to be much deeper. Not only chemical imbalance.

Seeker: What is the significance of a Guru and how does one know that one has found one?

Dadashreeji: *Even if you do not have a physical Master or a physical Guru, you have Google in your hand. So, you always refer to Google for something. That says that by the state* *of mind, you want someone to guide you. You always want someone to refer to, ask for. So for practical things you need Google or anyone who is your senior, teacher or professor. So when it comes to spiritual upliftment, when it comes to spiritual growth, definitely you need someone to guide you. You can't just go through books and read and feel that you have evolved. Today, you are spiritually enlightened. You can't declare yourself like that. It's liking writing an exam and giving marks to your own paper. It doesn't happen like that. At the same time, if you have a mobile number and if you keep calling your own mobile number, who is going to pick it up? No one. So there should be someone on the other side and the other person is what we call as the Master or spiritual Guide. You can name him anything. His role is to help you to grow in life. That's the only way it should be and every Master who is realized, who really experiences Truth in Himself, is going to serve you. He is not going to expect you to serve Him. So a true Master sees that he is able to serve you or make you grow so that you experience the beauty of life, the real side of life. That's how it should go ahead.*

As for the second part, there are different phases that you go through in life. If for example, in a confined state of mind, when you see your Master, if you have blocked yourself then you wouldn't be able to see that side of the person. If you open your mind or you talk to your heart, you would get that answer immediately without any pause. So if your heart is awakened, the answer is immediate and instant. If you work through your mind, it is going to take time because with your mind you would never find a perfect Master or even a perfect human being, because mind is always going to judge people. Mind doesn't have the quality of faith, so mind will never have faith on a Master. It's only the heart that has that quality, so we keep telling people not to try to have faith on any Master or on Me, because mind will never believe it. Accept yourself as it is. If you have found a master, accept Him as it is. Internally you connect and experience Him and then you will know what's exactly in it for you to move ahead. Even sitting here, you can close your eyes and you can just talk to yourself. It's your inner voice. Inner voice may tell you to wait for some time, wait for a few months or years. The right time will come when you will know your Master or you'll find a picture or a form. But you definitely need a Master. I am very much clear with it because in life, for everything you need some person to Guide, then why not here in spiritual life.

Seeker: What are the symptoms to know that our spiritual journey has begun?

Dadashreeji: *A very important sign at the beginning of spiritual growth (I am not saying that you've started growing but even the inclination to move towards spirituality) is that you start helping people. You start helping people automatically and this is what comes in the third phase of fulfillment where you feel that you go out and help someone, randomly maybe ,or someone asks you to help them and you go out to help them so you become somehow socially connected to that person. Only with one intention, to help, and that help is unconditional with no motive behind it. You just go out and help this person— if you see that, it means that time has come for you to grow automatically in a spiritual plane and then the search begins. What is more? What is next? Because even socially helping, you stop somewhere, that is also not completing. So you* *will need someone to guide you to explain what is the real essence of this life. And then you club your growth and social contribution together and that completes your journey of life.*

Seeker: How do you know that you are growing?

Dadashreeji: *Everyone is doing meditation or chanting or performing homas. There are a lot of things people do. The first sign to know that you are growing is when you start understanding others. The moment you start understanding others that means you are growing. So even if you are an atheist or a non-believer in God but still you understand the opposite person, that means you are spiritually growing. In spiritual growth, there is nothing like God and Master. It's just a flow of journey, and it's only intention or purpose is to seek that Truth. And, you move towards it. The form of a Master will only come to take you towards that end. Nothing more than that. It's your journey and you have to move towards it and your Master who is realised knows it very well how to take you ahead. He is not going to refer to books or a page number because he is in that state. He will understand you very well, and with every person, there will be a different unique delivery. Today what we have shared is a general idea about spiritual plane. But individually, when we speak, it is only a unique thing that will come for your own growth and then you walk on your path accordingly. So life is beautiful, you just have to flow with it. And spiritual journey, again it's internal. It's not external where you go with a tag on your shirt that says that I follow this Master or this Baba or this saintly being. These are all stories and we tell very categorically to our people that it's your internal state, nothing to do about public field or to tell people. Just flow with*

• • •

this. Very nice times are going to come in the future. When you walk on this path, you will be witnessing it.

Dadashreeji: *Being in the human plane, I had a lot of questions, questions about how to treat and help people around. I couldn't stand pain and wanted to help people, to take them forward, and this journey, this questioning itself, took me towards a different side of life when I started exploring, because my initial belief in life was very scientific and logical, practical. I need to see it if it is there. With that state of mind, I started my journey and then I had some mystical experiences which I try to avoid telling people because mystical side seems to be a very dreamy achievement for other people because people say it happened to you, but it did not happen to us that's why you are like that and we are not. But I would say that for me the journey was very simple and with the presence of Masters who came and guided me at that time. Those Masters were not physically here but were in different forms. Then around 2009-2010, I could experience the entire shift in my internal state itself wherein human mind got transferred into a Divine mind. And I say Divine mind because it involves everyone, it expresses only unconditional Love and there is internal freedom. I experience that compassion for everyone all the time, and when I am talking to you or others, I don't see that separation between us that was there before. So my understanding changed entirely by 2009 when I saw everything is one. There is no difference at all, and whatever we are interacting about is in that awareness. I am aware of the fact that we are One, and at the same time,*

I am playing my role of guiding few people. That's the only thing that is happening. With the presence of Mahavataar Babaji, in 2006, things started changing for me, and today , this is how I am, and it was entirely by the Divine guidance that I could move ahead. Today I am here just to interact and help you understand what it is all about. I think it's a journey and we'll flow together in this part of the journey.

Seeker: Did you find your Guru or did your Guru find you?

Dadashreeji: *I'll say both.*

Seeker: I believe nobody can find a Guru.

Dadashreeji: *For me it was a thought, an emotional craving that I needed someone to guide me, and at the same time, the path was on and the presence of Babaji was spontaneous.*

Seeker: In one word what would it be?

Dadashreeji: *Both.*

Seeker: I heard you and I was very impressed. I have multiple questions. All of us here are very successful people in different business or professions. But are we all successful because of our karma or past karma? This is number one. All of us must be at some level of spirituality. Level 1, 2, 3, or 4. Definitely we are at some level. Everyone is doing something good due to which they are successful and we are trying to do better. But my question is that some people become very successful as our Prime Minister Modi, going from a tea-seller to Prime Minister, and I believe that he is a very Divine person to be

• • •

able to control 120 crore people and successfully completing everything that he says. At the same time, his family is living a very simple life; they are very normal people. Is it because of present karma or past karmas or their luck?

Dadashreeji: *Luck and past life karma are one and the same. There's no difference here. Every person does carry destiny when you take birth in human life. You do carry all your past collected karmas and it comes in the form of destiny, and then you apply it throughout your life so everything that you have achieved is a result of past life karmas you did. At the same time, I would highlight that destiny does not confine your growth. It does not say that you are going to achieve only this much. There is always a possibility to go beyond your destiny. And that, all of you can achieve. In one of our spiritual sessions of Bodh, we do talk about 'destiny' that if you see human life as 100%, destiny plays a part of only 20%. Not entirely 100%. So your life is ruled by 20% of past life, and 70% is what you do today. And, that's why we strongly believe that with whatever you are doing today, you can change your destiny. And, everything can be transformed into much better state and there is no limitation to it. You have to keep exploring yourself. Don't stop growing. No one is going to stop your growth. No Divine being. No God, no Master is going to say – don't grow. Everyone wants, Nature wants, in fact, that you grow in your life. It is you who stop growing because of your judgements and ideas. So even if you take Modi for an example, definitely he got this post because of his past life, but how he is managing it today is going to decide the future of his own Self and the country. So, both are very very important. We can't push everything and say that it is because of past life. I say that because of this life you have got today. Keep*

• • •

working hard and everything will be there for you. So we want you to move ahead. We believe in doing actions. Without action, there is no Grace. So you have to act first. You can't just close your eyes and then imagine that God will come and He is going to change everything. You have to do and then He will give you His result.

Seeker: Dadashreeji, suffering is so real. I feel that it stops the growth. Can we eradicate suffering?

Dadashreeji: *Definitely, it can be eradicated and this is the time, in fact, to remove all that pain which you are referring to, and we as a team can work towards it and many other people are working towards it. Someone before gave an example of Modiji and many other like-minded people, and other spiritual Masters – everyone is working towards it to take suffering out of human consciousness, and that's possible and that will happen and that's how the journey of this era is going to be in the future. So it's very much possible, and we say only one thing here – to move away from your suffering connect to your Higher Self. Connect to your inner voice. That's the only solution which will be there for everyone here onwards. So connect with it, we are here to help and things will be all right very soon. But we as a team are working very confidently and very aggressively, in fact, to remove that pain from human consciousness and that will happen.*

Seeker: Even physical diseases, such as cancer, can they be terminated?

Dadashreeji: *Exactly. The cause of everything is underlying deep in your consciousness. If you access it and try to work on* *that, everything outwardly will change and we as a team are working towards it. As a doctor, we are also doing simultaneous research of our own activities. So we do scientific research also, which gives us a good feedback on what happens when we do the ShaktiPravaah process and what happens to the brain. In that, we have studied for more than three months, and we have seen a good change in human brain. So we are working towards it. You work towards it. We together can work towards it. And, I am very happy that you felt for others and are asking in what way you can help others. Thank you so much.*

Seeker: Even when we understand the pain of other people, sometimes that does not help us enough. For example, if the child comes home hungry and the mother hasn't cooked any food, even if the child understands, his hunger will not go away. What does the child do then?

Dadashreeji: *You have to accept that no one's pain or growth is going to be compromised. In this situation, if the boy feels hungry, this hunger is going to help that boy or child to grow in future. He has to take that in a positive manner. And, I have seen this happening in many families. In a family where the father drinks a lot of alcohol and comes home and starts shouting at his children's mother, the child decides at that young age that I am not going to do the same. So this situation is negative and bad, but he has decided to become a much better, positive person, so hunger would give a lesson to this child that when you grow, you see that nobody is sleeping without food, that you provide something for them. So in every opportunity of pain, there is a growth behind it. So I see even suffering as positive as it helps you* *to move forward in life. Everything is going to be much more positive and beneficial in the future.*

Seeker: What is the connection between having faith in the Guru and spirituality? For instance, Sai Baba is my Guru and whenever I have any problem, I say I leave it to you, and I get relaxed. Is this an element of spirituality or just pushing the burden on Guru?

Dadashreeji: *Action is something that you have to do so I would say you do all your actions, all your efforts, just convey and express from your side, and then leave it to your Master that – "Sai, I have done everything from my side as much as a human being or a human mind can do. Now I am leaving the result to you. You take care of it." This is the way to move forward and that will, in fact, help you grow, so faith should not make you handicapped as if you're really not doing anything and you stop thinking, because mind is a good instrument. It is entirely up to you how you use it. So in your mind if only positivity comes, it's only Sai and about Divinity. At the same time, if you are able to interact in the practical world also that's more than enough. So. do your actions and leave it to Sai then. But in this episode also of passing the burden on Sai, how I look at it is that you are at least interacting with your Divine which is very important even if it has pain, that's fine but he is there in your thought, and that in fact you should take care of and always grow with this thought in the future.*

An Evening with Dadashreeji in Mumbai, 2016

• • •

You must all be made aware

that your birth on this planet

itself was caused by

'Divine Will',

empowering you to attain

the 'Highest'

in this very lifetime.

\- Dadashreeji

Epilogue

What connects you to the Divine instantly

and strongly is 'Love'.

When you connect through Love,

you find the Divine is within you.

- Dadashreeji

Only Love can Change the World

Dear Friends,

Once I was asked, "Despite many years of hard work in life, as a result or as a gift, what do we get at the end?"

I replied, "Express your life in two words, summarizing all the experiences that you have had till now!"

He replied in a brittle voice – "Pain and dejection!"

The reason I am mentioning this here is to help you realize, what is it that we are looking for in life. It may not be your story, but do we get what we truly need? If you are aiming for hatred, violence, injustice, and pain, you can continue with whatever you are doing in life. However, if you are looking for the opposite of these, you need to consciously work towards them. Otherwise in the current world scenario, it is very easy to drift away from the true essence of life.

As long as the innocent, weak, and vulnerable, like children, women, the poor, and the elderly, are suffering and are being mistreated, something important is missing in this world for everyone. Will money, philosophy, advanced technology, knowledge, or religion end the suffering? All of these are limited due to the barriers of language, religion, country, culture. and exclusive access. Being discriminative, many people fail to receive transforming benefits from these. The available tools fall short of the vision of One World, One Community, and One Truth. It leads one to search for something far more, something that is universal to 'know and experience,' and yet works effectively beyond these limiting factors.

The answer lies deep within your heart. Just feel it once. When the body is relaxed and mind is calm, you experience the presence of 'that' powerful energy - Love. An incessant flow of bliss which is all about bonding, caring, giving, surrendering, and union. All other philosophies, knowledge, rituals, meditation, siddhis, mantras remain ineffective in transforming your false nature into a transcendental one. All these are effective only when they are followed and practised with Love.

History, repeatedly and loudly, has expressed the need of Love through many evolved spiritual Masters and Messengers. Enlightened Ones and mystics are bound to fall from their elevated level of awareness due to material bondage, simply because they lack Divine Love within. The proponent of Advait (Non-Dualism) philosophy, Adi Shankaracharya, towards the end of his journey shared the Truth as – the heart cannot be purified without the Love for the Divine. He called himself a Rasik – one who only enjoys the bliss of Divine Love. St. Francis of Assisi says, "Where there is hatred, let me sow Love." The human mind operating in a confined dimension is unable to fathom this Truth. Some treat this only as a positive thought and talk highly about it, but again do not actually walk on this path. Somehow, we trivialize Love and do not include it as the most essential element in our daily lives. Martin Luther King, Jr. once said, "Love is the only force capable of transforming an enemy into a friend." If that is so, why not transform your fallen false 'being' into a Higher True Self?

Come out of your shell! Free yourself, breathe deep, and dive into the real world of Love. This is the path of Love - Maitri propounded by the wise ones. Maitri is a 'State of Love for the Divine'. You are merged with your Inner Divine. You see Love within and in everything you come in contact with. Everything seems perfect; as work of the Divine. The Love that you have within, would be seen in others as well. You see 'all' as a part of the 'One Love'. Your consciousness expands, integrating all as ONE, which were separate earlier. You give and grow with Love. You realize, Love is not a concept but an experience! Hence, remember, only Love can truly change you and the world. Love alone can lead you to attaining Truth, Liberation, and real God.

Love and Blessings!
Dadashreeji

Life Positive Magazine, July 2018

There are so many ways and means for

spiritual transformation.

Appoint me as one of your guides…

I will be there for you at every step of your evolution.

-Dadashreeji

About

The MaitriBodh Parivaar

MaitriBodh is a path reconnecting you with your Higher sacred Self. It is an inner awakening, whereby one experiences an insightful bonding with the source of creation within. It radiates as 'unconditional Love and friendship' towards all beings.

The MaitriBodh Parivaar, founded by Divine Friend Dadashreeji is a socio-spiritual organization, a family of friends bonded by a common mission to develop, nurture, and strengthen the human bond of friendship and Love.

The vision of the MaitriBodh Parivaar is to establish Love in everyone's heart through human Transformation with the help of true knowledge and Divine intervention to attain One World, One Community, and One Truth.

The MaitriBodh Parivaar's work is aimed at transforming humanity through self-realization and selfless service, thereby preparing humanity to enter the new era of universal Peace and Love.

ShantiKshetra Premgiri Ashram

A Centre of Transformation & Excellence inspired and blessed by Supreme Master Mahavataar Babaji and Divine Friend Dadashreeji. ShantiKshetra Premgiri Ashram, as the name suggests, is a serene place located at the foothills of the Bhimashankar Mountains in Karjat, Raigad district of Maharashtra in India. As one enters the Centre, warmth and Love engulfs all, the root of which lies in the loving energy of a core group of disciples and volunteers. With passion in their hearts and humility in conduct, they have surrendered in Selfless Service to humanity, and welcome all with open arms – as one large loving family.

The key areas of the ShantiKshetra Premgiri Ashram are Shaktipeetham, the Energy Centre Temple, which represents the centre of cosmic power, the sacred abode of Divine Mother, Adishakti Mahakaali and the ancient form of Shivling Mahakaaleshwar, and DhyaanManthan Kshetra – the Meditation Hall.

Today, this place has developed as an abode for those who desire not only spiritual guidance, but also practical directions on living life with confidence and clarity. The premise resonates at a high powerful Divine vibration, enabling one to experience the Higher Truth of life.

MaitriBodh Activities

Since inception, the MaitriBodh Parivaar has been deeply involved in various spiritual programs, social projects, and youth initiatives.

Bodh Programs

At the core of MaitriBodh's activities are the Bodh programs that are centered on an individual's inner transformation and journey towards self-realization. Individuals or a group of individuals can enroll for the Bodh programs that start with Life Sutras, simple universal laws and teachings, going up to advanced spiritual techniques aimed to harmonize the mind, body, and soul.

Corporate Programs

Int'l Academy of Transformative Leadership partners with organizations to facilitate corporate evolution through human transformation and development. Customized interventions are designed in order to bring about sustained long-term organizational growth.

Social Projects

Under the banner of Peace Projects, the MaitriBodh Parivaar carries out various social initiatives –

Project Maitri Tejasvini:

Empowering women by offering various vocational and training workshops as well as job opportunities.

Sneh Sanskaar Gurukul:

Devoted towards providing education and holistic development through schools for underprivileged children.

Kamdhenu Gaushala:

Dedicated towards sheltering cows in a healthy and loving environment.

Aushadh Arogya Kendr:

Providing free health checkups and setting up medical camps in remote areas in collaboration with Hinduja Foundation.

Youth for Global Peace & Transformation:

The MaitriBodh Parivaar's enthusiastic youth wing takes up social, special projects based on the need of the community and society. Some of the social welfare events that are conducted are medical camps, cleanliness drives, environmental awareness, and anti-tobacco awareness events and counseling sessions to help youth achieve the desired transformation.

Earth Embrace:

A global campaign addressing the issue of climate change functioning on three important pillars: undertaking wellness activities for Mother Earth, creating global awareness, and instilling a sense of value for Mother Earth.

Prayer for Mother Earth

Today and now

I express my Love & care for you.

Forgive me for causing pain to You.

Let me protect and nurture You once again.

Let me heal Your wounds with my Love.

Love, Love, and only Love for You.

Universal Prayer

O Supreme! Almighty Creator of this Universe,
I surrender at your Lotus Feet.

O Creator, Nurturer, and Sustainer of our Life,
I surrender to the all-powerful Supreme Energy.

May I always surrender to the Supreme Being
whose presence manifests in every particle, each living being,
earth, water, air, fire, sky, and the mighty mountains.

May I always surrender to the Supreme Being who has
created me,
society, countries, and the world at large.

I surrender to the Supreme Presence in every being and form
that bonds with me through the expression of Love.

I surrender to the Supreme Energy, Supreme Presence,
Supreme Creator, Supreme Master, whose presence fills me with
Love, Peace, and Joy

O Supreme Master! True Friend!
I seek forgiveness for all my actions committed;
knowingly and unknowingly that may have caused pain.

O Divine, Liberate us!

*O Compassionate, Eternal Guru and friend who manifests as
pure Love,
liberate us from the suffering created by our thoughts,
words, and actions.*

*Seeking the forgiveness of all living and non-living beings,
O eternally-forgiving Supreme Soul, Supreme Master,
I humbly pray for your compassionate Grace!*

*O Supreme Bliss, Supreme Light, Supreme Peace,
Supreme Knowledge , Supreme Form of Love,
May I always be surrendered on the path towards Divine union,
the Highest Truth.*

*I humbly pray for the Grace and Love of the compassionate
Divine.*

|| ॐ Shanti Shanti Shanti ||

• • •

The simplest act of service brings

profound transformation in your life.

Through seva not just you,

but society itself is transformed.

You free yourself from all bindings.

Your consciousness is cleansed and purified within.

Divine Grace follows

and is showered on you abundantly.

\- Dadashreeji

I am Love.

You are Love.

Everything is Love.

- Dadashreeji